THE CONDITION OF TEACHING

A CARNEGIE FOUNDATION TECHNICAL REPORT

The Condition of Teaching

A STATE BY STATE ANALYSIS

C. EMILY FEISTRITZER

WITH A FOREWORD BY

ERNEST L. BOYER

[CF]

THE CARNEGIE FOUNDATION FOR THE

ADVANCEMENT OF TEACHING

5 IVY LANE, PRINCETON, NEW JERSEY 08540

Feistritzer, C. Emily
    The condition of teaching

    (A Carnegie Foundation technical report)
    Includes bibliographical references.
    1. Elementary school teachers — United States —
States - Statistics. 2. High school teachers — United
States — States — Statistics. I. Title. II. Series.
LB2832.2.F44 1983   373.11'009'22   83-15247
ISBN 0-931050-23-5

Copies are available from the
PRINCETON UNIVERSITY PRESS
3175 Princeton Pike
Lawrenceville, New Jersey 08648

CONTENTS

LIST OF TABLES

FOREWORD

By Ernest L. Boyer

The Carnegie Foundation for the Advancement of Teaching is completing a study of the American high school. During our investigation of secondary education we visited schools from coast to coast. Time and time again, we were reminded that excellence in education means excellence in teaching; that improving schools means improving the working conditions of those who meet with students every day.

We discovered in our study that teachers are troubled not only about salaries but about loss of status, the bureaucratic pressure, a negative public image, and the lack of recognition and rewards. To talk about recruiting better students into teaching without examining the current circumstances that discourage teachers is simply a diversion. The push for excellence in education must focus on those conditions that drove good teachers from the classroom in the first place, and this has to do with more than salaries.

In the great debate about public education, teachers are often blamed for what is wrong. And we hear much talk these days about recruiting better teachers. But to focus on future teachers misses an essential point. Whatever is wrong with American public schools cannot be fixed without the help of those teachers already in the nation's classrooms. Most of them will be there for years to come. And we must view today's teachers as part of the solution, not the problem.

Improving teaching in America means moving beyond the headlines and learning more about what actually goes on in schools today. What are the procedures by which teachers are admitted into teaching? What about salaries? How does teacher pay compare to that of other public employees and to corporate professions? Only when we discover where the profession of teaching is today can we design, with confidence, strategy for reform.

In this special report entitled, <u>The Condition of Teaching</u>, Emily Feistritzer has pulled together important information about teachers and about conditions that affect the schools. The facts presented in this report make clear that the teaching profession is in crisis. Poor students are going into teaching, teacher pay has actually declined in relation to other professionals and public employees. Credentialing is a mess and teachers do not receive adequate recognition and reward. The evidence supports the conclusion of Dan Lortie of the University of Chicago who wrote: "Real regard for those who taught has never matched professed regard."

Data in this report also vividly reveal that conditions of teaching vary greatly from one state to another. Salary schedules, for example, range from a high of over $34,000 in Alaska to a low of $14,500 in Mississippi. Clearly, while the problem of teaching can be talked about nationwide, the steps taken to strengthen the profession will vary significantly from place to place.

This special report also highlights the point that education and teaching cannot be viewed in isolation. Dr. Feistritzer places the school in the larger social context. The data highlight the fact that America is aging; that the school population is declining. Once again, however, the demographic pattern varies greatly from region to region and from state to state. Nevada, for example, grew 61 percent from 1972 to 1982, while New York, Rhode Island, and Pennsylvania actually lost population during this same period.

It is also significant that the racial and ethnic composition of the nation is changing. The white population increased by only 6 percent from 1970 to 1980 and dropped as a percentage of the total population. Blacks, the second largest racial group in the country, now represents about 12 percent of the total population. The fastest growing minority in the United States includes persons of Spanish origin, increasing in numbers from 9 million to over 14 million in just ten years.

Of special concern is the fact that black and Hispanic young people are precisely those with whom our schools have been least successful. Opportunity remains unequal and the failure to educate every young American to his or her full potential threatens the nation's social and economic health.

With fewer school age children, the commitment to white American families to public education may well decline. And while minority parents have a growing stake in education, historically they have had limited power to help the nation's schools. And yet, it is in the public schools where the education battle will be won or lost. Enrollment in non-public schools has been going down, not up. Today about 11 percent of America's school age children attend private elementary and secondary schools. In 1965, that figure stood at 13 percent. This means that the public schools are becoming more, not less, important.

This fact book is filled with statistics about schools and teachers. We present these data to help clarify the issues and improve the debate about the the future of education in the nation. But columns of numbers and statistical averages should not conceal the fact that behind the numbers there are people—teachers and students who must be supported in their work.

ERNEST L. BOYER
President
The Carnegie Foundation
for the Advancement of Teaching

INTRODUCTION

Aggregated national statistical averages mean little when it comes to education in the United States of America. State and local jurisdictions, not the federal government, control education in this country. The costs of education, the sources of revenue, the achievement scores of students, the scale of salaries for teachers, plus a host of other variables differ widely from state to state. We cannot understand the condition of teaching in this country, therefore, without knowing what is happening in 51 separate political entities—the 50 states and the District of Columbia.

The purpose of this report is to provide a state-by-state analysis of the condition of teaching in the United States. It analyzes changes over the past decade, for the country as a whole and for each state, in the following areas:

o General population shifts

o Elementary and secondary school enrollments, public and private

o Numbers of public elementary and secondary school teachers

o Public elementary and secondary school finance and its relationship to overall economic conditions—personal and per capita income, and sources of revenue—in each state

o Salaries of public elementary and secondary school teachers, as a percentage of total school expenditures and of total personal income, compared with salaries of other professionals and nonprofessional workers

o Certification requirements of the teaching profession

o Who is going into the teaching profession in this country and what that portends for the teaching force in the nation's public elementary and secondary schools in future years.

CHAPTER I

Population and Enrollment Trends

Two-thirds of the students enrolled in public elementary and secondary schools in the United States reside in not quite one-third (fourteen) of the states, and more than half of public elementary and secondary school teachers teach in those states (Table 1).

Internal migration from state to state, immigration from outside the nation's borders into the United States, and a declining birth rate at home from the late 1950s to the late 1970s—all three factors dramatically altered the makeup of the nation's classrooms over the past ten years. From 1972 to 1982, public elementary and secondary school enrollment dropped a total of 14.0 percent—from 45,960,736 to 39,505,691. But, while school enrollments fell, the U.S. population total rose by 10.6 percent, from 209,284,000 in 1972 to an estimated 231,534,000 in 1982. Persons between the ages of 5 and 17, who represented 24.7 percent of the total population in 1972, declined in numbers to 19.7 percent in 1982 (Table 2).[1]

Population Trends in the United States

Several states in the Western and Southern regions of the United States experienced a population explosion from 1972 to 1982 (Table 2). Nevada outdistanced all other states with an increase of 61.1 percent, followed by Wyoming, 44.7 percent; Arizona, 42.4 percent· Florida, 38.5 percent; Utah, 36.9 percent; Alaska, 34.4 percent; Texas, 29.9 percent; Colorado, 26.6 percent; Idaho, 26.5 percent; and New Mexico, 26.1 percent (Table 3).[2]

These same states, with the exception of Idaho, also showed the most rapid growth in total population over just the past three years. From 1979 to 1982,

TABLE 1. Public elementary and secondary school enrollment, number of teachers, average teacher salary and per-pupil expenditure, by state: 1982-83

State	Public Elementary and Secondary School Enrollment	Number of Teachers	Average Teacher Salary	Per Pupil Expenditure
United States	39,505,691	2,138,572	$20,531	$2,917
Alabama	724,037	39,400	$17,850	$1,546
Alaska	86,683	5,630	33,953	6,620
Arizona	546,000	28,856	18,849	2,603
Arkansas	437,021	23,505	15,176	2,093
California	3,958,775	170,397	23,555	2,490
Colorado	544,800	29,000	21,500	2,986
Connecticut	505,400	31,698	20,300	3,746
Delaware	92,645	5,344	20,665	4,008
District of Columbia	87,581	4,909	26,048	3,767
Florida	1,476,000	82,041	18,538	3,009
Georgia	1,045,900	57,016	17,412	2,369
Hawaii	161,874	8,124	24,796	3,213
Idaho	205,020	10,125	17,549	2,110
Illinois	1,875,199	104,249	22,618	3,201
Indiana	1,005,159	50,692	20,067	2,672
Iowa	496,300	31,013	18,709	3,147
Kansas	405,810	26,280	18,299	3,094
Kentucky	652,000	32,200	18,400	2,193
Louisiana	774,000	42,499	19,265	2,529
Maine	211,986	12,277	15,772	2,651
Maryland	699,136	37,746	22,786	3,486
Massachusetts	925,160	52,000	19,000	2,958
Michigan	1,761,906	77,206	23,965	3,648
Minnesota	718,662	40,643	22,296	3,157
Mississippi	461,000	24,842	14,285	2,076
Missouri	806,400	48,257	17,726	2,587
Montana	151,988	8,906	19,463	2,981
Nebraska	264,478	16,249	17,412	2,605
Nevada	151,100	7,442	20,944	2,311
New Hampshire	161,298	10,105	15,353	2,341
New Jersey	1,157,000	73,291	21,642	4,190
New Mexico	269,111	14,250	20,600	2,904
New York	2,693,100	163,100	25,100	4,302
North Carolina	1,104,220	56,459	17,836	2,680
North Dakota	116,569	7,499	18,390	3,055
Ohio	1,850,800	95,010	20,360	2,807
Oklahoma	580,832	33,900	18,110	2,792
Oregon	447,449	24,500	22,334	3,643
Pennsylvania	1,781,000	102,700	21,000	3,290
Rhode Island	137,538	8,758	23,175	3,792
South Carolina	604,600	32,080	16,380	2,016
South Dakota	123,625	7,974	15,595	2,386
Tennessee	827,857	39,233	17,425	2,124
Texas	2,982,000	166,800	19,500	2,299
Utah	369,338	14,889	19,677	2,128
Vermont	91,597	6,591	15,338	2,940
Virginia	975,717	56,892	18,707	2,740
Washington	738,571	34,497	28,413	2,887
West Virginia	375,126	22,001	17,370	2,480
Wisconsin	784,800	52,200	20,940	3,421
Wyoming	101,523	7,297	24,000	3,467

SOURCE: Selected data from The National Education Association, Estimates of School Statistics: 1982-83, (Washington: National Education Association, January 1983), pp. 30, 34, and 35.

TABLE 2. Total population and percentage of population of school age, by state: 1972 and 1982

Region and State	1972 Total Population (in thousands)	1972 Percentage of Total Population of School Age	1982 Total Population (in thousands)	1982 Percentage of Total Population of School Age	Percentage Change in Total Population from 1972 to 1982	Change in Percentage of Population of School Age from 1972 to 1982
United States	209,284	24.7	231,534	19.7	10.6	-5.0
New England						
Connecticut	3,070	24.9	3,153	18.8	2.7	-6.1
Maine	1,035	24.5	1,133	20.5	9.5	-4.0
Massachusetts	5,762	26.6	5,781	18.4	0.3	-8.2
New Hampshire	782	23.9	951	20.1	21.6	-3.8
Rhode Island	976	22.6	958	18.0	-1.8	-4.6
Vermont	463	25.1	516	20.2	11.4	-4.9
Mid Atlantic						
Delaware	574	25.6	602	19.4	4.9	-6.2
District of Columbia	744	21.5	631	14.4	-15.2	-7.1
Maryland	4,081	25.4	4,265	19.6	4.5	-5.8
New Jersey	7,337	24.3	7,438	19.2	1.4	-5.1
New York	18,352	23.6	17,659	18.7	-3.8	-4.9
Pennsylvania	11,905	24.1	11,865	18.8	-0.3	-5.3
Great Lakes						
Illinois	11,258	25.2	11,448	19.8	1.7	-5.4
Indiana	5,296	25.8	5,471	20.8	3.3	-5.0
Michigan	9,025	26.8	9,109	21.2	0.9	-5.6
Ohio	10,747	25.9	10,791	20.1	0.4	-5.8
Wisconsin	4,498	26.3	4,765	17.0	5.9	-9.3
Plains						
Iowa	2,861	25.5	2,905	19.3	1.5	-6.2
Kansas	2,256	24.9	2,408	18.4	6.7	-6.5
Minnesota	3,867	26.7	4,133	19.5	4.2	-5.2
Missouri	4,753	24.5	4,951	19.3	4.2	-5.2
Nebraska	1,518	25.0	1,586	19.3	4.5	-5.7
North Dakota	631	27.1	670	19.1	6.2	-8.0
South Dakota	677	26.9	691	19.8	2.1	-7.1
Southeast						
Alabama	3,540	25.9	3,943	21.4	11.4	-4.5
Arkansas	2,018	24.2	2,291	21.3	13.5	-2.9
Florida	7,520	21.1	10,416	17.6	38.5	-3.5
Georgia	4,807	25.0	5,639	21.7	17.3	-3.3
Kentucky	3,336	24.9	3,667	21.3	9.9	-3.6
Louisiana	3,762	27.2	4,362	21.9	15.9	-5.3
Mississippi	2,307	27.0	2,551	22.9	10.6	-4.1
North Carolina	5,296	24.6	6,019	20.3	13.7	-4.3
South Carolina	2,718	26.0	3,203	21.6	17.8	-4.4
Tennessee	4,088	24.1	4,651	20.4	13.8	-3.7
Virginia	4,828	24.4	5,491	19.5	13.7	-4.9
West Virginia	1,797	24.2	1,948	21.0	8.4	-3.2
Southwest						
Arizona	2,009	23.8	2,860	20.7	42.4	-3.1
New Mexico	1,078	28.2	1,359	21.9	26.1	-6.3
Oklahoma	2,657	23.3	3,177	19.6	19.6	-3.7
Texas	11,759	25.1	15,280	21.0	29.9	-4.1
Rocky Mountain						
Colorado	2,405	24.1	3,045	19.2	26.6	-4.9
Idaho	763	25.4	465	22.5	26.5	-2.9
Montana	719	26.4	801	19.7	11.4	-6.7
Utah	1,135	27.0	1,554	24.1	36.9	-2.9
Wyoming	347	25.9	502	21.9	44.7	-4.0
Far West						
California	20,585	23.9	24,729	18.5	20.1	-5.4
Nevada	547	23.4	881	19.0	61.1	-4.4
Oregon	2,195	23.5	2,649	19.6	20.7	-3.9
Washington	3,447	25.1	4,245	19.5	36.9	-2.9
Alaska	326	26.7	438	19.4	34.4	-7.3
Hawaii	828	24.3	994	19.4	20.0	-4.9

SOURCE: Selected data from the U.S. Department of Commerce, Bureau of the Census, Statistical Abstract of the United States: 1982-83, 103rd ed., (Washington: U.S. Government Printing Office, 1983), p. 12, U.S. Department of Commerce, Bureau of Economic Analysis, Commerce News, Report BEA #83-21, (Washington: U.S. Department of Commerce, May 1983), Table 4; computations from selected data in The National Education Association, Estimates of School Statistics: 1982-83, (Washington: National Education Association, January 1983), p. 30; and The National Education Association, Estimates of School Statistics: 1973-74, (Washington: National Education Association, 1974), p. 25.

Nevada's population grew by 15.2 percent, and that of Wyoming by 11.1 percent, Florida and Texas by 10.0 percent each, Utah by 9.7 percent, Arizona and Alaska by 8.4 percent each, Colorado by 6.9 percent, California by 6.3 percent, and New Mexico by 6.1 percent.

Only three states and the District of Columbia lost population in the last decade: The District of Columbia's population decreased by 15.3 percent, New York's by 3.8 percent, Rhode Island's by 1.8 percent, and Pennsylvania's by 0.3 percent. The District of Columbia also showed the sharpest decline in population (3.8 percent) from 1979 to 1982. Michigan lost a greater proportion of its residents, 1.5 percent, than any other state over the same three years. Two other industrial states, Pennsylvania and Ohio, each registered a slight decline of 0.1 percent in total population from 1979 to 1982.[3]

Regionally, population shifts are dramatic. Two decades ago, 30.7 percent of the total population lived in the South, 15.6 percent in the West, 28.8 percent in the North Central States, and 24.9 percent in the Northeast. By 1981, the proportion living in the South had increased to 33.6 percent, and the proportion in the West rose to 19.3 percent. The proportion of the population living in the North Central region had dropped to 26.7 percent; the proportion living in the Northeast dropped to 21.5 percent.

Clearly, the population of the United States is shifting from the large industrial states in the Northeast and North Central regions to the "Sun Belt" areas of the South and Far West. The reason usually given is that people perceive better economic opportunities there. But other factors are strong, including: 1) declining birth rates over the past fifteen years creating a larger population of "older" people who are migrating to warmer climates; and 2) immigration into the United States, especially from Mexico, Cuba, and Central America, by people who stay where they land—in the South and West.

Six of the ten states that grew the most in the past decade also showed the greatest increase of people 65 years of age and older (Table 3). Nevada's over-65 population went up 112.5 percent. Florida's increased by 70.4 percent; Alaska's, by 64.7 percent; New Mexico's, by 62.9 percent; Arizona's, by 60.7 percent; and Utah's, by 40.0 percent. Overall, the percentage of residents living in all 50 states who were 65 and older in 1980 varied from 17.3 percent in Florida to 2.9 percent in

TABLE 3. States ranked by percentage change in total resident population and their percentage increase in population 65 years of age and older: 1970 to 1980

	State	Percentage Change in Resident Population from 1970 to 1980	Percentage Change in Population 65 Years of Age and Older (rank in parenthesis) 1970 to 1980
1.	Nevada	63.43	112.15 (1)
2.	Arizona	53.12	90.67 (2)
3.	Florida	43.43	70.35 (4)
4.	Wyoming	41.81	24.06 (28)
5.	Utah	37.96	40.03 (10)
6.	Idaho	32.39	37.76 (13)
7.	Alaska	32.17	64.71 (5)
8.	Colorado	30.72	31.79 (22)
9.	New Mexico	27.82	62.94 (6)
10.	Texas	27.05	38.21 (11)
11.	Oregon	25.84	33.61 (19)
12.	Hawaii	25.32	73.25 (3)
13.	New Hampshire	24.74	32.01 (20)
14.	Washington	21.01	33.98 (18)
15.	South Carolina	20.39	50.41 (7)
16.	Georgia	19.10	40.82 (9)
17.	Arkansas	18.85	31.23 (24)
18.	California	18.84	34.08 (17)
19.	Oklahoma	18.22	25.35 (27)
20.	Tennessee	16.93	34.77 (15)
21.	North Carolina	15.55	45.48 (8)
22.	Louisiana	15.43	31.58 (23)
23.	Virginia	14.95	38.05 (12)
24.	Vermont	14.93	23.76 (29)
25.	Mississippi	13.70	30.34 (25)
26.	Kentucky	13.67	21.62 (37)
27.	Montana	13.36	22.55 (32)
28.	Maine	13.14	22.54 (34)
29.	Alabama	12.95	34.95 (14)
30.	West Virginia	11.79	22.61 (31)
	United States	11.41	27.30
31.	Delaware	8.62	34.74 (16)
32.	Maryland	7.45	31.86 (21)
33.	Minnesota	7.12	17.30 (40)
34.	Wisconsin	6.50	16.12 (42)
35.	Nebraska	5.72	11.73 (48)
36.	Indiana	5.66	22.55 (32)
37.	North Dakota	5.61	21.89 (36)
38.	Missouri	5.12	15.56 (43)
39.	Kansas	5.08	15.10 (45)
40.	Michigan	4.24	21.16 (38)
41.	South Dakota	3.63	13.77 (47)
42.	Iowa	3.13	10.71 (49)
43.	Illinois	2.75	15.19 (44)
44.	New Jersey	2.69	23.34 (30)
45.	Connecticut	2.49	26.25 (26)
46.	Ohio	1.32	17.18 (41)
47.	Massachusetts	0.84	14.23 (46)
48.	Pennsylvania	0.56	20.37 (39)
49.	Rhode Island	−0.30	22.04 (35)
50.	New York	−3.75	10.18 (50)
51.	District of Columbia	−15.77	4.51 (51)

SOURCE: National Education Association, Rankings of the States 1982, (Washington: National Education Association, 1982), pp. 7, 9.

Alaska. The proportion of a state's population over 65 is significant in the context of generating revenue for schools and in determining overall expenditures within a state.

There was little variation among the states in their proportion of school-aged population. In 1982, persons aged 5 to 17 ranged from 24.1 percent of Utah's total population to 17.0 percent in Wisconsin and 14.4 percent in the District of Columbia. The national average for school-aged persons in the states was 24.7 percent in 1972. That dropped to an estimated 19.7 percent in 1982.

Population by Sex

The U.S. population as a whole and state by state in all age groups except the elderly remains virtually evenly divided at about 50 percent male and 50 percent female. For persons aged 65 and older, the percentage of women is greater.

Racial and Ethnic Composition of the Population
in the United States

One of the most significant demographic changes centers on the nation's racial and ethnic composition. The percentage of black Americans increased from 11.1 percent in 1970 to 11.7 percent in 1980; of American Indians from 0.4 percent to 0.6 percent, of Asian and Pacific Islanders from 0.8 percent to 1.5 percent, and of persons of Spanish origin from 4.5 percent to 6.4 percent. From 1970 to 1980, the black population increased by 17.3 percent. There were also increases in the population of American Indians, by 71 percent; Chinese, 85.3 percent; Filipinos, 125.8 percent; Japanese, 18.5 percent; and Korean, 412.8 percent.[4]

The white population in the United States increased by only 6 percent from 1970 to 1980. Still the overwhelming majority, it nevertheless dropped, as a percentage of total population, from 87.4 percent in 1970 to 83.2 percent in 1980.[5]

Blacks, the second largest racial group in this country, represented about 12 percent of the total population in 1980. Fifty-three percent of all blacks, about the same proportion as a decade ago, live in the South. In 1980, the District of Columbia had the greatest proportion of blacks, 70.3 percent; followed by

Mississippi, 35.2 percent; South Carolina, 30.4 percent; Louisiana, 29.4 percent; Georgia, 26.8 percent; and Alabama. 25.6 percent.

Although the West recorded the smallest proportion of blacks of any region in both 1970 and 1980, it was the only region that experienced an increase in the percentage of black residents—from 7.5 percent in 1970 to 8.5 percent in 1980. The Northeast had a slight decline in its black population, from 19.0 percent in 1970 to 18.0 percent in 1980. The proportion of blacks in the North Central region remained about the same, 20.6 percent.[6]

The fastest growing minority group of significant size in the United States includes persons of Spanish origin. Their numbers increased by 61.0 percent—9,294,500 in 1970 to 14,609,000 in 1980. In both 1970 and 1980, more than 60 percent of the nation's Hispanics lived in California, Texas, and New York. California ranks first in the number of Hispanics—4.5 million (19.2 percent of the state's total population); followed by Texas, with 3.0 million (21.0 percent); and New York, 1.7 million (9.5 percent). Other states with large Hispanic populations include New Mexico, 37.0 percent; Arizona, 16.0 percent; and Colorado, 12.0 percent.[7]

The 1980 Census estimate of the composition of the U.S. population by race and persons of Spanish origin is presented in Tables 4 and 5.

Public Elementary and Secondary School Enrollment

Even though the overall population of the United States grew by 10.6 percent, enrollments in the nation's public elementary and secondary schools dropped 14.0 percent—from 46,960,736 in 1972-73 to an estimated 39,505,691 in 1982-83.[8]

The sharpest enrollment decline took place in public secondary schools, 17.9 percent from 1972-73 to 1982-83. Public elementary schools lost 11.1 percent of their pupils nationwide during the period (Tables 6, 7, and 8).

The largest enrollment drops for the decade occurred in the Mid-Atlantic and North Central regions. Fifteen states and the District of Columbia experienced declines of 20 percent or more: Delaware, 31.0 percent; Rhode Island, 27.5 percent; Connecticut, 25.0 percent; Pennsylvania, 24.6 percent; Maryland, 24.1 percent; South Dakota, 23.8 percent; Ohio, 23.4 percent; Iowa, 23.2 percent;

TABLE 4. Percentage distribution of population by racial and ethnic group, by state: 1980

Region and State	Total Population	White	Black	American Indian, Eskimo, Aleut	Asian, Pacific Islander	Other
United States	226,504,825	83.2	11.7	0.6	1.5	3.0
New England						
Connecticut	3,107,576	90.2	7.0	0.1	0.6	2.2
Maine	1,124,660	98.7	0.3	0.4	0.3	.4
Massachusetts	5,737,037	93.5	3.9	0.1	0.9	1.7
New Hampshire	920,610	98.9	0.4	0.1	0.3	.2
Rhode Island	947,154	94.7	2.9	0.3	0.6	1.5
Vermont	511,456	99.1	0.2	0.2	0.3	.2
Mid Atlantic						
Delaware	595,225	82.1	16.1	0.2	0.7	.9
District of Columbia	637,651	26.9	70.3	0.2	1.0	1.6
Maryland	4,216,446	74.9	22.7	0.2	1.5	.7
New Jersey	7,364,158	83.2	12.6	0.1	1.4	2.7
New York	17,557,288	79.5	13.7	0.2	1.8	4.8
Pennsylvania	11,866,728	89.8	8.8	0.1	0.5	.8
Great Lakes						
Illinois	11,418,461	80.8	14.7	0.1	1.4	3.0
Indiana	5,490,179	91.2	7.6	0.1	0.4	.8
Michigan	9,258,344	85.0	12.9	0.4	0.6	1.0
Ohio	10,797,419	88.9	10.0	0.1	0.4	.6
Wisconsin	4,705,335	94.4	3.9	0.6	0.4	.7
Plains						
Iowa	2,913,387	97.4	1.4	0.2	0.4	.5
Kansas	2,363,208	91.7	5.3	0.7	0.6	1.6
Minnesota	4,077,148	96.6	1.3	0.9	0.7	.6
Missouri	4,917,444	88.4	10.5	0.3	0.5	.4
Nebraska	1,570,006	94.9	3.1	0.6	0.4	.9
North Dakota	652,695	95.8	0.4	3.1	0.3	.4
South Dakota	690,178	92.6	0.3	6.5	0.3	.3
Southeast						
Alabama	3,890,061	73.8	25.6	0.2	0.2	.2
Arkansas	2,285,513	82.7	16.3	0.4	0.3	.3
Florida	9,739,992	84.0	13.8	0.2	0.6	1.5
Georgia	5,464,265	72.3	26.8	0.1	0.4	.3
Kentucky	3,661,433	92.3	7.1	0.1	0.3	.2
Louisiana	4,203,972	69.2	29.4	0.3	0.6	.5
Mississippi	2,520,638	64.1	35.2	0.2	0.3	.2
North Carolina	5,874,429	75.8	22.4	1.1	0.4	.3
South Carolina	3,119,208	68.8	30.4	0.2	0.4	.3
Tennessee	4,590,750	83.5	15.8	0.1	0.3	.2
Virginia	5,346,279	79.1	18.9	0.2	1.2	.6
West Virginia	1,949,644	96.2	3.3	0.1	0.3	.2
Southwest						
Arizona	2,717,866	82.4	2.8	5.6	0.8	8.4
New Mexico	1,299,968	75.1	1.8	8.1	0.5	14.5
Oklahoma	3,025,266	85.9	6.8	5.6	0.6	1.2
Texas	14,228,383	78.7	12.0	0.3	0.8	8.2
Rocky Mountain						
Colorado	2,888,834	89.0	3.5	0.6	1.0	5.8
Idaho	943,935	95.5	0.3	1.1	0.6	2.4
Montana	786,690	94.1	0.2	4.7	0.3	.6
Utah	1,461,037	94.6	0.6	1.3	1.0	2.4
Wyoming	470,816	95.1	0.7	1.5	0.4	2.3
Far West						
California	23,668,562	76.2	7.7	0.9	5.3	10.0
Nevada	799,184	87.5	6.4	1.7	1.8	2.7
Oregon	2,632,663	94.6	1.4	1.0	1.3	1.6
Washington	4,130,163	91.5	2.6	1.5	2.5	2.0
Alaska	400,481	77.0	3.4	16.0	2.0	1.6
Hawaii	965,000	33.0	1.8	0.3	60.5	4.4

SOURCE: Selected data from the U.S. Department of Commerce, Bureau of the Census, "Race of the Population by States: 1980," 1980 Census of Population, (Washington: U.S. Government Printing Office, July 1981), PC80-S1-3, pp. 6, 8, 9.

TABLE 5. Percentage distribution of Hispanic population by state.

Region and State	Total Population	Hispanic Total	Mexican	Puerto Rican	Cuban	Other Spanish	Non Hispanic
United States	226,545,805	6.4	3.9	.9	.4	1.3	93.6
New England							
Connecticut	3,107,576	4.0	.1	2.8	.2	.8	96.0
Maine	1,124,660	.4	.1	.1	–	.2	99.6
Massachusetts	5,737,037	2.5	.1	1.3	.1	.9	97.5
New Hampshire	920,610	.6	.1	.1	–	.3	99.4
Rhode Island	947,154	2.1	.1	.5	.1	1.4	97.9
Vermont	511,456	.6	.1	.1	–	.4	99.4
Mid Atlantic							
Delaware	594,338	1.6	.3	.8	.1	.5	98.4
District of Columbia	638,333	2.8	.5	.2	.2	1.9	97.2
Maryland	4,216,975	1.5	.3	.2	.1	.9	98.5
New Jersey	7,364,823	6.7	.2	3.3	1.1	2.1	93.3
New York	17,558,072	9.5	.2	5.6	.4	3.2	90.5
Pennsylvania	11,863,895	1.3	.2	.8	–	.3	98.7
Great Lakes							
Illinois	11,426,518	5.6	3.6	1.1	.2	.7	94.4
Indiana	5,490,224	1.6	1.0	.2	–	.3	98.4
Michigan	9,262,078	1.8	1.2	.1	–	.4	98.2
Ohio	10,797,630	1.1	.5	.3	–	.3	98.9
Wisconsin	4,705,767	1.3	.9	.2	–	.2	98.7
Plains							
Iowa	2,913,808	.9	.6	–	–	.2	99.1
Kansas	2,363,679	2.7	2.1	.1	–	.4	97.3
Minnesota	4,075,970	.8	.5	–	–	.2	99.2
Missouri	4,916,686	1.1	.7	.1	–	.3	98.2
Nebraska	1,569,825	1.8	1.4	–	–	.3	98.2
North Dakota	652,717	.6	.4	–	–	.2	99.4
South Dakota	690,768	.6	.3	–	–	.2	99.4
Southeast							
Alabama	3,893,888	.9	.5	.1	–	.3	99.1
Arkansas	2,286,435	.8	.5	–	–	.2	99.2
Florida	9,746,324	8.8	.8	1.0	4.8	2.2	91.2
Georgia	5,463,105	1.1	.5	.1	.1	.4	98.9
Kentucky	3,660,777	.7	.4	.1	–	.3	99.3
Louisiana	4,205,900	2.4	.7	.1	.2	1.4	97.6
Mississippi	2,520,638	1.0	.6	–	–	.3	99.0
North Carolina	5,881,766	1.0	.6	.1	.1	.3	99.0
South Carolina	3,121,820	1.1	.5	.1	.1	.3	98.9
Tennessee	4,591,120	.7	.4	.1	–	.3	99.3
Virginia	5,346,818	1.5	.5	.2	.1	.8	98.5
West Virginia	1,949,644	.7	.3	–	–	.3	99.3
Southwest							
Arizona	2,718,215	16.2	14.6	.1	–	1.4	83.8
New Mexico	1,302,894	36.6	17.9	.1	–	18.5	63.4
Oklahoma	3,025,290	1.9	1.3	.1	–	.5	98.1
Texas	14,229,191	21.0	19.3	.2	.1	1.4	79.0
Rocky Mountain							
Colorado	2,889,964	11.8	7.2	.1	.1	4.4	88.2
Indiana	943,935	3.9	3.0	–	–	.8	96.1
Montana	786,690	1.3	.8	–	–	.4	98.7
Utah	1,461,037	4.1	2.6	.1	–	1.4	95.9
Wyoming	469,557	5.2	3.4	.1	–	1.7	94.8
Far West							
California	23,667,902	19.2	15.4	.4	.3	3.2	80.8
Nevada	800,493	6.7	4.1	.2	.5	2.0	93.3
Oregon	2,633,105	2.5	1.7	.1	–	.7	97.5
Washington	4,132,156	2.9	2.0	.1	–	.8	97.1
Alaska	401,851	2.4	1.1	.2	–	.9	97.6
Hawaii	964,691	7.4	.9	2.0	–	4.4	92.6

SOURCE: U.S. Department of Commerce, Bureau of the Census, "Persons of Spanish Origin by State: 1980," 1980 Census of Population, (Washington, U.S. Government Printing Office, August 1982), PC80-S1-7, pp. 6, 7.

TABLE 6. Enrollments in public elementary and secondary schools and percentage change, by state: 1972-73 and 1982-83

State	Public/Elementary Secondary Enrollment 1972-73	1982-83	Percentage Change from 1972-73 to 1982-83
50 States and D.C.	45,960,736	39,505,691	-14.0
Alabama	783,383	724,037	-7.6
Alaska	84,685	86,683	2.4
Arizona	522,748	546,000	4.4
Arkansas	457,768	437,021	-4.5
California	4,500,978	3,958,775	-12.0
Colorado	574,248	544,800	-5.1
Connecticut	673,529	505,400	-25.0
Delaware	134,317	92,645	-31.0
District of Columbia	139,918	87,581	-37.4
Florida	1,642,045	1,476,000	-10.4
Georgia	1,084,402	1,045,900	-3.6
Hawaii	178,000	161,874	-9.0
Idaho	184,663	205,020	11.0
Illinois	2,354,562	1,875,199	-20.3
Indiana	1,220,569	1,005,159	-17.6
Iowa	646,408	496,300	-23.2
Kansas	491,232	405,310	-17.4
Kentucky	714,632	652,000	-8.8
Louisiana	845,840	774,000	-8.5
Maine	247,448	211,986	-14.3
Maryland	920,896	699,136	-24.1
Massachusetts	1,202,000	925,160	-23.0
Michigan	2,193,270	1,761,906	-19.7
Minnesota	909,814	718,662	-21.0
Mississippi	526,344	461,000	-12.4
Missouri	1,030,008	806,400	-21.7
Montana	172,056	151,988	-11.7
Nebraska	329,192	264,478	-19.6
Nevada	131,673	151,000	14.7
New Hampshire	168,094	161,298	-4.0
New Jersey	1,497,867	1,157,000	-22.8
New Mexico	280,472	269,111	-4.1
New York	3,494,805	2,693,100	-22.9
North Carolina	1,158,549	1,104,220	-4.7
North Dakota	141,535	116,569	-17.6
Ohio	2,415,348	1,850,800	-23.4
Oklahoma	607,083	580,832	-4.3
Oregon	477,587	447,449	-6.3
Pennsylvania	2,361,285	1,781,000	-24.6
Rhode Island	189,693	137,538	-27.5
South Carolina	623,778	604,600	-3.1
South Dakota	162,398	123,625	-23.8
Tennessee	883,383	827,857	-6.3
Texas	2,833,009	2,982,000	5.3
Utah	305,9116	369,338	20.7
Vermont	106,517	91,597	-14.0
Virginia	1,069,345	975,717	-8.8
Washington	790,502	738,571	-6.6
West Virginia	409,952	375,126	-8.5
Wisconsin	995,223	784,800	-21.1
Wyoming	85,391	101,523	18.9

SOURCE: Computed from selected data in the National Education Association, Estimates of School Statistics: 1973-74, (Washington: National Education Association, 1974), p. 25; and Estimates of School Statistics: 1982-83, (Washington: National Education Association, January 1983), p. 30.

TABLE 7. Enrollment in public elementary schools and percentage change, by state: 1972-73 to 1982-83

State	Public Elementary School Enrollment 1972-73	Public Elementary School Enrollment 1982-83	Percentage Change from 1972-73 to 1982-83
United States	26,811,059	23,786,241	-11.1
Alabama	407,737	386,828	-5.1
Alaska	51,373	48,669	-5.3
Arizona	373,776	382,000	2.2
Arkansas	239,918	235,773	-1.7
California	2,745,737	2,712,572	-1.2
Colorado	311,530	310,000	-0.5
Connecticut	478,528	337,300	-29.5
Delaware	71,950	47,751	-33.6
District of Columbia	83,869	48,772	-41.8
Florida	884,398	794,530	-10.2
Georgia	686,601	649,800	-5.3
Hawaii	96,700	86,925	-10.1
Idaho	91,847	118,243	28.7
Illinois	1,471,576	1,288,218	-12.5
Indiana	657,764	530,563	-19.3
Iowa	357,597	263,300	-26.4
Kansas	277,481	245,500	-11.5
Kentucky	450,230	432,667	-3.9
Louisiana	510,888	550,000	7.6
Maine	177,393	146,848	-17.2
Maryland	507,973	342,576	-32.6
Massachusetts	675,000	613,974	-9.0
Michigan	1,168,731	917,337	-21.5
Minnesota	469,994	358,302	-23.8
Mississippi	302,220	253,600	-16.1
Missouri	737,884	554,792	-24.8
Montana	116,980	107,017	-8.5
Nebraska	180,058	149,811	-16.8
Nevada	72,756	81,640	12.2
New Hampshire	96,819	93,539	-3.4
New Jersey	972,483	728,910	-25.0
New Mexico	144,391	149,900	3.8
New York	1,878,260	1,308,600	-30.3
North Carolina	799,709	770,863	-3.6
North Dakota	94,319	80,647	-14.5
Ohio	1,469,582	1,117,300	-24.0
Oklahoma	333,144	332,832	-0.1
Oregon	278,863	275,329	-1.3
Pennsylvania	1,224,959	880,100	-28.2
Rhode Island	116,937	69,201	-40.8
South Carolina	386,532	421,100	8.9
South Dakota	110,361	85,718	-22.3
Tennessee	543,500	590,423	8.6
Texas	1,545,777	1,906,050	23.3
Utah	163,724	221,521	35.3
Vermont	65,515	48,261	-26.3
Virginia	665,310	600,386	-9.8
Washington	412,792	381,414	-7.6
West Virginia	229,425	224,769	-2.0
Wisconsin	574,918	445,000	-22.6
Wyoming	45,250	59,120	30.6

SOURCE: Computed from selected data in The National Education Association, Estimates of School Statistics: 1973-74, (Washington: National Education Association, 1974), p. 25; and Estimates of School Statistics: 1982-83, (Washington: National Education Association, January 1983), p. 30.

TABLE 8. Enrollment in public secondary schools and percentage change, by state: 1972-73 to 1982-83

State	Public Secondary School Enrollment 1972-73	Public Secondary School Enrollment 1982-83	Percentage Change from 1972-73 to 1982-83
United States	19,149,677	15,714,450	-17.9
Alabama			
Alaska	375,646	337,209	-10.2
Arizona	33,312	38,014	14.1
Arkansas	148,972	164,000	10.1
California	217,850	201,248	-7.6
	1,755,241	1,246,203	-29.0
Colorado			
Connecticut	262,718	234,800	-10.6
Delaware	195,001	168,100	-13.8
District of Columbia	62,367	44,894	-28.0
Florida	56,049	38,809	-30.8
	763,647	681,470	-10.8
Georgia			
Hawaii	397,801	396,100	-0.4
Idaho	81,300	74,949	-7.8
Illinois	92,816	86,777	-6.5
Indiana	882,986	586,981	-33.5
	562,805	474,596	-15.7
Iowa			
Kansas	288,811	233,000	-19.3
Kentucky	213,751	160,310	-25.0
Louisiana	264,402	219,333	-17.0
Maine	334,952	224,000	-33.1
	70,055	65,138	-7.0
Maryland			
Massachusetts	412,923	356,560	-13.6
Michigan	527,000	311,186	-40.9
Minnesota	1,024,539	844,569	-17.6
Mississippi	439,820	360,360	-18.1
	224,124	207,400	-7.5
Missouri			
Montana	292,124	251,608	-13.9
Nebraska	55,076	44,971	-18.3
Nevada	149,134	114,667	-23.1
New Hampshire	58,917	69,460	17.9
	71,275	67,759	-4.9
New Jersey			
New Mexico	525,384	428,090	-18.5
New York	136,081	119,211	-12.4
North Carolina	1,616,545	1,384,500	-14.4
North Dakota	358,840	333,357	-7.1
	47,216	35,922	-23.9
Ohio			
Oklahoma	946,142	733,500	-22.5
Oregon	273,939	248,000	-9.5
Pennsylvania	198,724	172,120	-13.4
Rhode Island	1,136,326	900,900	-20.7
	72,756	68,337	-6.1
South Carolina			
South Dakota	237,246	183,500	-22.6
Tennessee	52,037	37,907	-27.1
Texas	339,883	237,434	-30.1
Utah	1,287,232	1,076,000	-16.4
	142,192	147,817	4.0
Vermont			
Virginia	41,002	43,336	5.7
Washington	404,035	375,331	-7.1
West Virginia	377,710	357,157	-5.4
Wisconsin	180,527	150,357	-16.7
Wyoming	420,305	339,800	-19.2
	40,141	42,403	5.6

SOURCE: Computed from selected data in The National Education Association, Estimates of School Statistics: 1973-74, (Washington: National Education Association, 1974), p. 25; and Estimates of School Statistics: 1982-83, (Washington: National Education Association, January 1983), p. 30.

Massachusetts, 23.0 percent; New York, 22.9 percent; New Jersey, 22.8 percent; Missouri, 21.7 percent; Minnesota, 21.0 percent; Wisconsin, 21.1 percent; Illinois, 20.3 percent; and District of Columbia, 37.4 percent.

These states are the same ones that either suffered net losses in total population or grew more slowly than states in other regions.

Only seven states, all in the South and the West, increased their enrollments in public elementary and secondary schools in the past decade. Utah had the largest increase: 20.7 percent overall, representing a 35.3 percent increase in enrollment in public elementary schools and one of 4.0 percent in public secondary schools. Utah's total population increased by 36.9 percent during this period.

Wyoming had the second highest increase in public school enrollment from 1972-73 to 1982-83. Its 18.9 percent reflected a 30.6 percent increase in elementary schools and 5.6 percent increase at the secondary level. Wyoming's total population grew by 44.7 percent during this decade.

The seven states registering increases in public elementary and secondary school enrollments are shown in Table 9.

Four of the seven states posting increases in their total public school enrollments--Utah, Wyoming, Nevada and Arizona--showed growth at both the elementary and secondary levels.

TABLE 9. Percentage change in states with enrollment increases in public elementary and secondary schools, ranked: 1972-73 to 1982-83

State	In total public elementary and secondary school enrollment	In elementary school enrollment	In secondary school enrollment
Utah	20.7	35.3	4.0
Wyoming	18.9	30.6	5.6
Nevada	14.7	12.2	17.9
Idaho	11.0	28.7	-6.5
Texas	5.3	23.3	-16.4
Arizona	4.4	2.2	10.1
Alaska	2.4	-5.3	14.1

SOURCE: Computed from selected data in The National Education Association, Estimates of School Statistics: 1973-74, (Washington: National Education Association, 1974), p. 25; and Estimates of School Statistics: 1982-83, (Washington: National Education Association, January 1983), p. 30.

While Idaho and Texas realized an approximate 25 percent increase in public elementary school enrollment between 1972-73 and 1982-83, their secondary school enrollment decreased. Enrollment in the public secondary schools in Texas dropped 16.4 percent, while enrollment at the secondary level in Idaho fell 6.5 percent. Alaska experienced just the reverse: an increase in secondary school enrollment and a decrease at the elementary school level. Alaska's public secondary school enrollment jumped 14.1 percent while enrollment in its public elementary schools declined 5.3 percent.

Racial and Ethnic Enrollment in Public Elementary
and Secondary Schools

In 1970, blacks accounted for 14.9 percent of the total public elementary and secondary school enrollment. Hispanics represented 5.1 percent, and American Indians and Orientals represented 0.5 percent each. In 1980, black non-Hispanic students comprised 16.1 percent of the enrollment total, followed by Hispanics at 8.0 percent, Asians or Pacific Islanders at 1.9 percent, and American Indian or Alaskan Natives at 0.8 percent.

The total number of students enrolled in public elementary and secondary schools in the United States has decreased since 1970, but the number of minority students has increased steadily. In the fall of 1980, they accounted for 26.7 percent of public school enrollment, compared with 21.0 percent in 1970.

While minorities represent 17 percent of the total U.S. population, they make up more than 26 percent of the total school-age population. It is projected that by 1990, minorities will constitute 20 to 25 percent of the total population and more than 30 percent of school enrollment.[9]

Minority enrollments vary significantly from state to state. The District of Columbia has the highest, at 96.4 percent (93.4 percent black, 2.0 percent Hispanic and 1.0 percent Asian or Pacific Islander). Of the 48 contiguous states, New Mexico has the highest proportion of minority students at 57.0 percent (46.5 percent Hispanic), followed by Mississippi, with 51.6 percent (51.0 percent black).

Black elementary and secondary public school enrollment is highest in the Southern states: Mississippi, 51.0 percent; South Carolina, 42.8 percent; Louisiana,

41.5 percent; Georgia, 33.5 percent; Alabama, 33.1 percent; Maryland, 30.6 percent; North Carolina, 29.6 percent; Virginia, 25.5 percent; Tennessee, 24.0 percent; Florida, 23.4 percent; and Arkansas, 22.5 percent.

Other states having black student enrollments above the national average of 16.1 percent include: Delaware, 25.9 percent; Illinois, 20.9 percent; New Jersey, 18.5 percent; Michigan, 17.9 percent; and New York, 17.9 percent (Table 10). Maine has the smallest percentage (0.9) of minority students in its public schools.

As might be expected, Hispanics represent the largest minority group enrolled in states near the Mexican border. Their numbers are influenced significantly by the influx of illegal aliens. An estimated 6 million illegal aliens already are in the United States, with 2 million more expected in 1983.[10]

New Mexico's elementary and secondary school enrollment consists of 46.5 percent Hispanic children and 7.8 percent American Indians. Texas has a minority enrollment of 45.9 percent, with 30.4 percent Hispanic and 14.4 percent black. California's public elementary and secondary school enrollment is 42.9 percent minority: 25.3 percent Hispanic, 10.1 percent black, 6.6 percent Asian or Pacific Islander, and 0.8 percent American Indian or Alaskan Native.

Arizona rounds out those states with a large Hispanic enrollment. Of its 33.7 percent minority students, 24.2 percent are Hispanic, 4.2 percent are black, 4.1 percent are American Indian or Alaskan Native, and 1.1 percent are Asian or Pacific Islander.

Private Elementary and Secondary School Enrollment

Nearly 11 percent of America's children 5 to 17 years of age who are enrolled in school attend private elementary and secondary schools. Of the 4,961,755 students enrolled in private schools in 1980, only 16.0 percent were in nonreligiously affiliated schools. The remaining 84.0 percent enrolled in religiously affiliated schools—63.2 percent of them in Catholic schools.[11]

This represents a drop in private school enrollment. In 1965, 13.0 percent of elementary and secondary students were enrolled in private schools. Of the 6,304,800 students then attending private schools, 94.6 percent were in religiously affiliated schools (Table 11).[12]

TABLE 10. Racial and ethnic distribution of public elementary and secondary school enrollment, by state: Fall 1980

State	Total	White Non-Hispanic	Minority	Black Non-Hispanic	Hispanic	American Indian Alaskan Native	Asian or Pacific Islander
50 States and D.C.	100.0	73.3	26.7	16.1	8.0	0.8	1.9
Alabama	100.0	66.4	33.6	33.1	.1	.2	.2
Alaska	100.0	71.6	28.4	3.9	1.6	20.6	2.3
Arizona	100.0	66.3	33.7	4.2	24.2	4.1	1.1
Arkansas	100.0	76.5	23.5	22.5	.3	.4	.3
California	100.0	57.1	42.9	10.1	25.3	.8	6.6
Colorado	100.0	77.9	22.1	4.6	15.3	.5	1.7
Connecticut	100.0	83.0	17.0	10.2	5.8	.1	.9
Delaware	100.0	71.2	28.8	25.9	1.8	.1	.9
District of Columbia	100.0	3.6	96.4	93.4	2.0	0	1.0
Florida	100.0	67.8	32.2	23.4	7.9	.1	.8
Georgia	100.0	65.7	34.3	33.5	.3	0	.5
Hawaii	100.0	24.8	75.2	1.4	2.0	.2	71.4
Idaho	100.0	91.8	8.2	.5	4.6	2.1	1.0
Illinois	100.0	71.4	28.6	20.9	6.1	.1	1.5
Indiana	100.0	88.0	12.0	9.9	1.5	.1	.5
Iowa	100.0	95.9	4.1	2.2	.8	.2	.9
Kansas	100.0	87.3	12.7	7.8	3.0	.6	1.2
Kentucky	100.0	90.9	9.1	8.7	.1	0	.3
Louisiana	100.0	56.6	43.4	41.5	.8	.4	.8
Maine	100.0	99.1	.9	.3	.1	.2	.3
Maryland	100.0	66.5	33.5	30.6	.9	.2	1.8
Massachusetts	100.0	89.3	10.7	6.2	3.3	.1	1.1
Michigan	100.0	78.7	21.3	17.9	1.8	.8	.8
Minnesota	100.0	94.1	5.9	2.1	.7	1.6	1.5
Mississippi	100.0	48.4	51.6	51.0	.1	.1	.4
Missouri	100.0	85.2	14.8	13.6	.5	.1	.5
Montana	100.0	87.9	12.1	.3	1.2	9.8	.8
Nebraska	100.0	89.5	10.5	5.6	1.9	2.2	.8
Nevada	100.0	81.1	18.9	9.5	5.2	2.0	2.2
New Hampshire	100.0	98.7	1.3	.5	.4	0	.4
New Jersey	100.0	71.6	28.4	18.5	8.0	.1	1.7
New Mexico	100.0	43.0	57.0	2.2	46.5	7.8	.6
New York	100.0	68.0	32.0	17.9	12.0	.2	2.0
North Carolina	100.0	68.1	31.9	29.6	.2	1.6	.4
North Dakota	100.0	96.5	3.5	.5	.5	1.8	.7
Ohio	100.0	85.3	14.7	13.1	1.0	.1	.6
Oklahoma	100.0	79.2	20.8	9.3	1.6	9.1	.8
Oregon	100.0	91.5	8.5	2.1	2.6	1.7	2.2
Pennsylvania	100.0	85.1	14.9	12.4	1.5	.2	.7
Rhode Island	100.0	91.8	8.2	4.7	2.1	.3	1.1
South Carolina	100.0	56.5	43.5	42.8	.2	.1	.4
South Dakota	100.0	92.1	7.9	.2	.2	7.2	.3
Tennessee	100.0	75.5	24.5	24.0	.1	0	.4
Texas	100.0	54.1	45.9	14.4	30.4	.2	1.1
Utah	100.0	92.7	7.3	.5	3.5	1.8	1.5
Vermont	100.0	99.0	1.0	.3	.1	.1	.5
Virginia	100.0	72.5	27.5	25.5	.5	.1	1.4
Washington	100.0	85.9	14.1	3.4	4.0	3.0	3.7
West Virginia	100.0	95.7	4.3	3.9	.1	0	.3
Wisconsin	100.0	90.7	9.3	6.2	1.5	.9	.7
Wyoming	100.0	92.5	7.5	.7	5.3	1.0	.4

SOURCE: The National Center for Education Statistics, The Condition of Education: 1983, (Washington: U.S. Government Printing Office, 1983), p. 22.

TABLE 11. Private elementary and secondary school enrollment and percentage in non-religiously affiliated schools, by state: Fall 1980

State	Private School Enrollment as Percentage of Total Elementary/Secondary Enrollment	Private Elementary/Secondary School Enrollment	Percentage of Private School Enrollees in Non-religiously Affiliated Schools
United States	10.8	4,961,755	16.0%
1. Delaware	19.0	23,374	18.6
2. Hawaii	18.4	37,147	35.4
3. District of Columbia	17.5	21,203	35.4
4. Pennsylvania	17.4	402,058	21.9
5. Louisiana	17.0	158,921	19.0
6. New York	16.8	579,670	12.2
7. Rhode Island	16.8	29,875	8.8
8. Wisconsin	16.4	162,361	3.7
9. New Jersey	15.6	229,878	10.2
10. Illinois	15.0	349,463	7.4
11. Connecticut	14.3	88,404	23.8
12. Missouri	13.0	126,319	7.0
13. Maryland	12.4	106,447	17.7
14. Nebraska	12.1	38,574	3.5
15. Ohio	12.1	268,357	5.3
16. Florida	12.0	204,988	24.4
17. Massachusetts	11.9	138,33	20.5
18. California	11.1	513,709	20.1
19. New Hampshire	11.0	20,721	28.4
20. Minnesota	10.5	88,966	5.0
21. Michigan	10.2	211,871	7.5
22. Mississippi	9.5	50,116	60.5
23. Iowa	9.4	55,227	2.4
24. Kentucky	9.4	69,728	15.8
25. Indiana	8.7	100,234	7.4
26. North Dakota	8.4	10,659	14.7
27. South Dakota	7.8	10,898	16.4
28. Tennessee	7.7	71,617	29.0
29. Alabama	7.6	62,669	39.3
30. Kansas	7.5	33,889	10.4
31. South Carolina	7.4	49,619	49.1
32. Arizona	7.3	40,261	27.2
33. Maine	7.3	17,540	45.6
34. Vermont	7.3	7,555	43.2
35. Georgia	7.2	82,505	53.9
36. Virginia	6.9	75,069	35.7
37. Washington	6.9	55,950	15.9
38. New Mexico	6.2	18,027	28.7
39. Colorado	6.1	35,250	20.6
40. Oregon	5.7	27,828	14.6
41. North Carolina	4.9	58,078	42.4
42. Texas	4.9	148,534	12.1
43. Montana	4.7	7,668	12.1
44. Nevada	4.2	6,599	14.3
45. Alaska	4.2	3,800	14.9
46. Arkansas	4.0	18,423	28.2
47. West Virginia	3.2	12,608	6.7
48. Wyoming	3.0	3,036	25.0
49. Idaho	2.8	5,839	6.5
50. Oklahoma	2.7	16,335	13.6
51. Utah	1.6	5,555	33.5

SOURCE: Selected data from The National Center for Education Statistics, The Condition of Education: 1983, (Washington: U.S. Government Printing Office, 1983), pp. 16, 18.

States vary considerably in the proportion of their students enrolled in private schools. The range extends from 19.0 percent in Delaware to under 2.0 percent in Utah.

Twenty states, plus the District of Columbia, had more than 10.0 percent of their elementary and secondary pupils enrolled in private schools in 1980. Delaware led, with 19.0 percent; followed by Hawaii, with 18.4 percent; and the District of Columbia, with 17.5 percent.

States having the smallest proportion of their elementary and secondary school students enrolled in private schools in 1980 included Utah, 1.6 percent; Oklahoma, 2.7 percent; Idaho, 2.8 percent; Wyoming, 3.0 percent; and West Virginia, 3.2 percent.

States with the highest percentage of elementary and secondary private school students enrolled in nonreligiously affiliated schools in 1980 were Mississippi, 60.5 percent; Georgia, 53.9 percent; South Carolina, 49.1 percent; Maine, 45.6 percent; Vermont, 43.2 percent; and North Carolina, 42.4 percent.

CHAPTER II

Number of Public School Teachers

There is a paradox in the relationship between American teachers and their students. Public elementary and secondary school enrollment dropped 14.0 percent in the past decade, yet the number of public elementary and secondary school teachers increased by 1.4 percent (Chart 1). Further, the total instructional staff (including classroom teachers, principals, supervisors, librarians, guidance and psychological personnel, and related instructional workers) increased by 2.4 percent from 1972-73 to 1982-83.[13]

In 1972-73, public school systems across the United States employed 2,108,846 teachers to instruct 45,960,875 public elementary and secondary school students (Table 12). In 1982-83, an estimated 2,138,572 teachers were teaching the 39,505,691 students enrolled in the nation's public elementary and secondary schools.

Declining enrollments in the nation's elementary and secondary schools--both public and private--have been due primarily to a drop in the U.S. birth rate during the 1960s and most of the 1970s. Children of the baby-boom era after World War II kept school enrollments high throughout the 1950s and 1960s. As a result, demand for teachers was high. But when the baby-boom children were graduated from high school, fewer children were around for all the new schools that had been built and all the teachers that had been hired.

The most obvious result was a lower student-teacher ratio. Class sizes shrank. The average student-teacher ratio in public elementary and secondary schools in the United States dropped from 22:1 in 1972-73 to 18:1 in 1982-83. The average number of elementary students per teacher fell from 23 to 20 as the aver-

CHART I.   State by state comparison of percentage of
            change in enrollments and numbers of teachers in
            public elementary and secondary schools, 1972-73
            and 1982-83

SOURCE: Tables 7, 8, 17, and 19

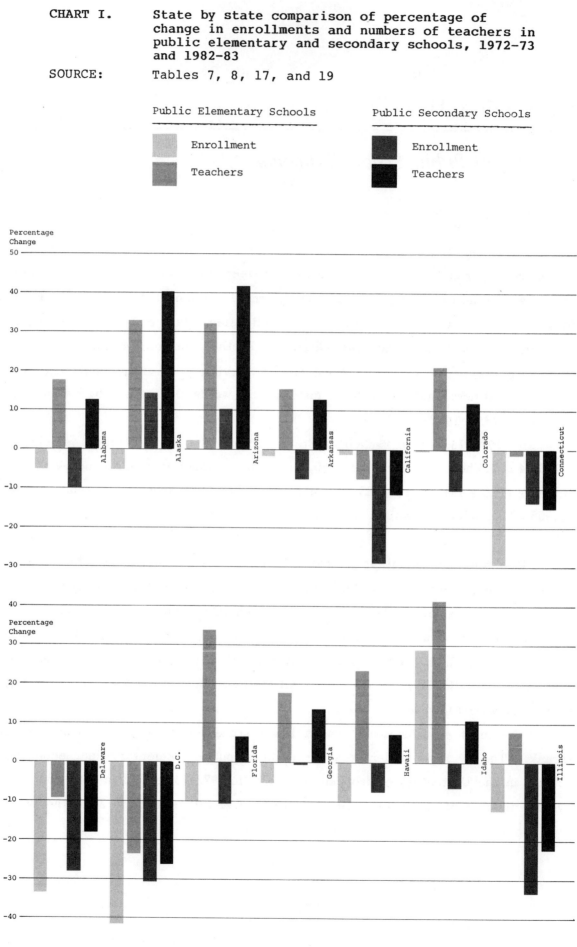

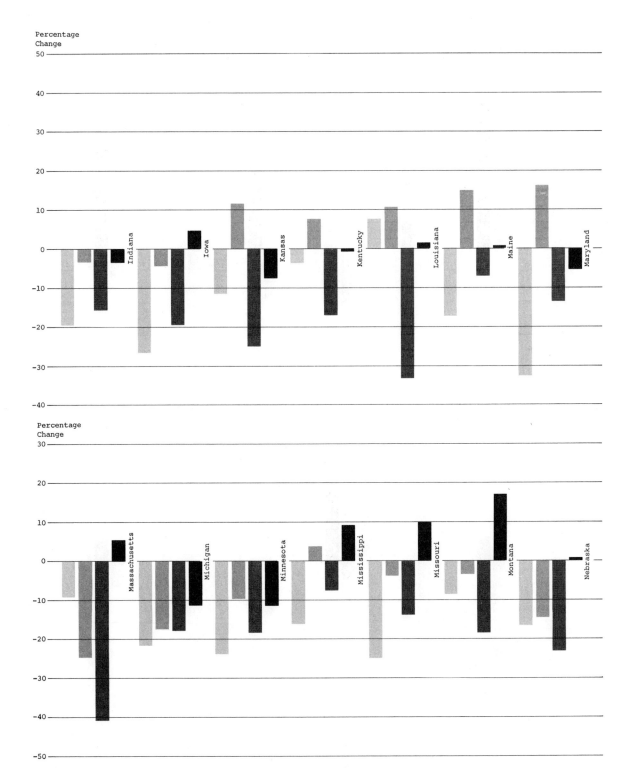

Percentage
Change

Indiana

Iowa

Kansas

Kentucky

Louisiana

Maine

Maryland

Percentage
Change

Massachusetts

Michigan

Minnesota

Mississippi

Missouri

Montana

Nebraska

CHART I.
(Continued)

SOURCE:

State by state comparison of percentage of change in enrollments and numbers of teachers in public elementary and secondary schools, 1972–73 and 1982–83

Tables 7, 8, 17, and 19

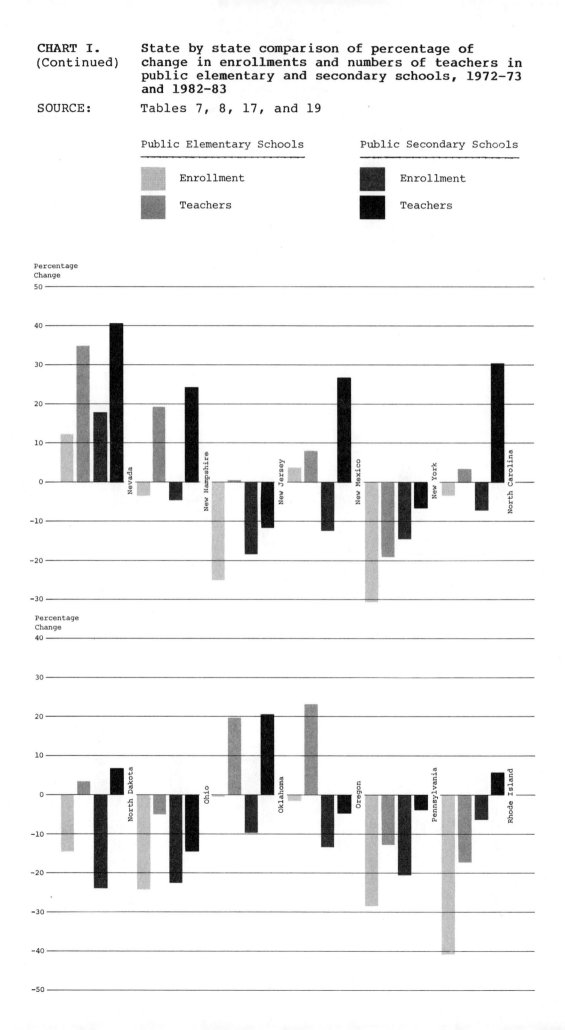

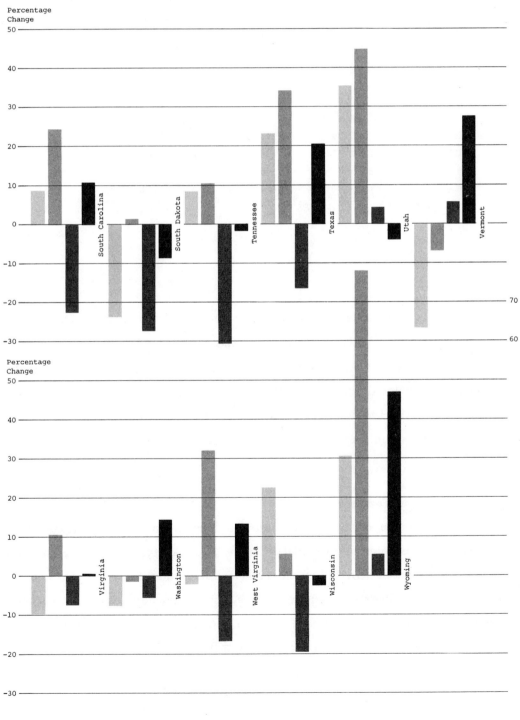

Percentage
Change
50

40

30

20

10

0

-10

-20

-30

70

60

South Carolina

South Dakota

Tennessee

Texas

Utah

Vermont

Percentage
Change
50

40

30

20

10

0

-10

-20

-30

-40

Virginia

Washington

West Virginia

Wisconsin

Wyoming

TABLE 12. Public elementary and secondary enrollment and numbers of teachers with percent changes: 1972–73 to 1982–83

School Year	Average Daily Attendance	Percent change over 1972-73	Total Classroom Teachers	Percent Change over 1972-73
1972–73	45,134,236	----	2,108,846	----
1973–74	44,911,989	−0.4	2,138,284	1.4
1974–75	44,442,070	−1.4	2,170,623	2.9
1975–76	43,975,419	−2.5	2,170,623	3.9
1976–77	43,610,204	−3.3	2,186,301	3.7
1977–78	42,938,327	−4.8	2,197,461	4.2
1978–79	41,934,900	−7.0	2,205,913	4.6
1979–80	41,063,696	−8.9	2,208,667	4.7
1980–81	40,059,905	−11.1	2,202,841	4.5
1981–82	39,457,587	−12.5	2,157,827	2.3
1982–83	38,578,972	−14.4	2,138,572	1.4

SOURCE: Selected data from The National Education Association, Estimates of School Statistics: 1982–83, (Washington: National Education Association, January 1983), p. 12.

age number of secondary students per teacher declined even further, from 20 to 16.

In spite of the shrinking class size, the number of teachers continued to increase over the decade. Reasons include: 1) More teachers were needed to accommodate exceptional children after the 1975 passage of Public Law 94-142, the Education for All Handicapped Act; and 2) the addition of elective and "frill" courses to the curriculum required a greater number of teachers.

The Typical American Teacher

One popular conception of the American teacher as an old, spinsterish "school-marm" bears no resemblance to reality (Table 13). A "typical" American teacher today would be a woman still in her thirties who had taught for 12 years, mostly in her present district. Over those dozen years, she would have returned to her local college or university often enough to acquire enough credits for a master's degree. She would be married and the mother of two children. She would be white and not

TABLE 13. Selected characteristics of public school teachers, United States: Spring 1961 to Spring 1981

Item	1961	1966	1971	1976	1981
Median age (years):					
All teachers	41	36	35	33	37
Men	34	33	33	33	38
Women	46	40	37	33	36
Race (percent):					
Black	(a)	(a)	8.1	8.0	7.8
White	(a)	(a)	88.3	90.8	91.6
Other	(a)	(a)	3.6	1.2	0.7
Sex (percent):					
Men	31.1	31.1	34.3	32.9	33.1
Women	68.7	69.0	65.7	67.0	66.9
Married status (percent):					
Single	22.3	22.0	19.5	20.1	18.5
Married	68.0	69.1	71.9	71.3	73.0
Widowed, divorced, or separated	9.7	9.0	8.6	8.6	8.5
Highest degree held (percent):					
Less than bachelor's	14.6	7.0	2.9	0.9	0.4
Bachelor's	61.9	69.6	69.6	61.6	50.1
Master's or six years	23.1	23.2	27.1	37.1	49.3
Doctor's	0.4	0.1	0.4	0.4	0.3
Median years of teaching experience	11	8	8	8	12
Average number of pupils per class					
Elementary teachers, not departmentalized	29	28	27	25	25
Elementary teachers, departmentalized	(a)	(a)	25	23	22
Secondary teachers	28	26	27	25	23
Average number of hours in required school day	7.4	7.3	7.3	7.3	7.3
Average number of hours per week spent on all teaching duties	47	47	47	46	46
Average number of days of classroom teaching in school year	(a)	181	181	180	180
Average annual salary of classroom teacher (b)	$5,264	$6,253	$9,261	$12,005	$17,209

(a) Data not available
(b) Includes extra pay for extra duties

NOTES: Data are based upon sample surveys of public school teachers. Because of rounding, percent may not add to 100.0

SOURCE: Selected data from The National Education Association, <u>Status of the American Public School Teacher</u>, (Washington: National Education Association, 1982), pp. 15-19.

politically active. Her formal political affiliation, if she had one, would be with the Democratic Party. She would teach in a suburban elementary school staffed largely by women, although, in all likelihood, the school principal would be male. She would have about twenty-three pupils in her class. Counting her after-hours responsibilities, she would put in a work week slightly longer than that of the average blue-collar worker in industry, but bring home a pay check that would be slightly lower.[14]

Age: Most of today's teachers in elementary and secondary schools are just entering middle age. Compared with teachers in 1970, they are both older and younger. The number of new or recently hired teachers has been reduced because of declining enrollments. Staff cuts fell heavily on young teachers: In 1970, almost 17 percent of all teachers were under 25. Today, that figure is around 8 percent. There also are fewer older teachers in the teaching force. Many districts have encouraged teachers to retire early to avoid layoffs. In 1970, almost 14 percent of all teachers were over 55. Today, teachers over 55 constitute only about 8 percent of the total teaching force.[15]

Experience: The typical classroom teacher, having taught for 12 years, with 10 of them in her current district, could be considered a top performer at the peak of her career. But another, less flattering interpretation is that opportunities for further development and substantive salary increases could be over. Many teachers, in fact, view themselves as having reached the plateau where they are stranded. They see no real opportunities for growth or reward. A number of teachers report this as a major problem.[16]

Academic preparation: Teachers are a relatively experienced and nontransient lot. They also are going to school longer and getting more degrees. Today, almost half (49.3 percent) of the teachers in elementary and secondary schools have earned at least a master's degree. In some states, such as California, a master's degree is required to obtain a teaching license. This advanced level of training stands in sharp contrast to the way things were done 10 years ago. For example, in 1971, only slightly more than one-fourth (27.1 percent) of the teachers in schools in the

United States held an advanced degree. In 1950, a considerable number of normal school graduates had not received even a bachelor's degree.[17]

Sex: The great majority of the 1,176,711 public elementary school teachers in classrooms today are women. In 1982-83, there were 981,262 women teaching in elementary schools and approximately 195,449 men; as a result, the ratio of women to men in elementary schools remains high—as it has historically—at about 5 to 1. In secondary schools, there is a relative balance between men and women. The 1982-83 estimates showed 487,713 (53.6 percent) men and 474,148 (50.7 percent) women. Almost 75 percent of all these teachers are married.[18] Fewer men overall are choosing teaching today than a decade ago, and the percentage of women teaching in secondary schools is definitely on the rise. Generally, a secondary school teacher's salary is higher than that of an elementary teacher, and more prestige is associated with teaching in high school than in elementary school.

Ethnic background: If males are underrepresented in the teaching force, especially in elementary schools, so are minority groups. Almost 9 of every 10 teachers are white. It is estimated that blacks constitute 8.6 percent of the teaching force. The proportion of teachers from other minority groups is very small. Hispanics represent 1.8 percent of teachers in kindergarten through high school, and Asian American and American Indians represent less than 1 percent. There is great variation in the racial/ethnic distribution according to geographic location. Southern states have a much higher percentage of minority teachers than the national average, which is consistent with their share of the minority population.[19] Examples of states with large percentages of minority teachers include: Mississippi, 38.6 percent; Louisiana, 35.3 percent; Georgia, 27.6 percent; Alabama, 27.2 percent; and South Carolina, 26.1 percent. On the other hand, some non-Southern states fall short in their percentages of minority teachers, as measured against the size of their minority population and school enrollment. Examples of these states include New York, 7.8 percent; Colorado, 6.8 percent; Iowa, 1.1 percent; Minnesota, 0.8 percent; and South Dakota, 0.8 percent.

Where they teach: The basic administrative unit for the American school system is the local school district. There has been a continuing decrease in the number of districts as consolidations occurred to avoid duplication and conserve costs. In 1931, there were more than 127,000 school districts. Today there are slightly fewer than 16,000. These districts contain about 62,000 elementary schools and 24,500 secondary schools (including junior high and middle schools). Of the secondary schools, 21.8 percent have enrollments of between 1,000 and 2,499 students, and 26.5 percent have fewer than 300 students.

Only 11 percent of our teachers work in what is considered the inner core of a city while another 9 percent work elsewhere in urban areas. Almost two-thirds teach in a suburb (31 percent) or a small town (33 percent). Another 16 percent teach in schools characterized as rural.

Of the 2,138,572 teachers employed in K-12 schools in 1982-83, 1,176,711 were in elementary schools and 961,861 in secondary schools. In 1981, almost half of all teachers were categorized as strictly elementary (48.7 percent), nearly one quarter (23.1 percent) as middle or junior high school teachers, and the remainder (28.2 percent) as senior high school teachers.

A typical elementary school today has about 500 students, compared with almost 600 in 1973. Middle or junior high schools tend to enroll about 700 students and senior high schools about 1,200 students. The decline in student enrollment has been at the elementary school level and is just now beginning to affect secondary schools. Secondary schools probably will continue to get smaller over the next decade while numbers of students in elementary schools will grow somewhat.[20]

Classroom demand: Although classroom size diminished over the past decade at both the elementary and secondary levels, it appears that teacher-pupil ratios are beginning to edge upward again. Difficult economic conditions offer one explanation for the turnaround.

Teachers estimate the average number of hours in the required school day to be 7.3. Since they also estimate that they spend about 46 hours per week on teaching-related duties, it would appear that teachers spend beyond normal school hours an additional two hours each day on their teaching responsibilities. The average school year across the country is 180 teaching days.[21]

Job satisfaction: More than one-third of America's teachers report dissatisfaction with their current jobs. Twelve percent of them are very dissatisfied. Over half the teachers (55 percent) in a 1981 survey said they either certainly or probably would not become a teacher again.

This is a shocking increase in the number of dissatisfied teachers. Twenty years ago only 11 percent of teachers polled reported they certainly or probably would not choose teaching if they had it to do over again.

Public attitudes toward school and treatment of education by the media are reported by teachers as the number one and two variables contributing to job dissatisfaction. Salary ranks fourth, followed by status of teachers in the community.[22]

Number of Teachers

The number of teachers in public elementary and secondary schools in the United States rose 1.4 percent in the past decade because some states increased their teaching staffs significantly (Tables 14 and 15). Even though enrollment declined in 43 states and the District of Columbia, only 16 states and the District of Columbia reduced the total number of teachers in public elementary and secondary schools.

Percentage Changes in Numbers of Teachers

The District of Columbia lost over one-third of its public elementary and secondary school enrollment and dropped nearly one-fourth of its teachers from 1972-73 to 1982-83. Michigan had the highest percentage decline in total number of teachers of the 50 states—enrollment down by almost 20 percent (from 2,193,270 in 1972-73 to an estimated 1,761,906 in 1982-83) and teachers by 14.4 percent (from 90,218 to an estimated 77,206) in the decade.

Fifteen other states realized a decrease both in enrollment and in numbers of teachers from 1972-73 to 1982-83 (Table 16).

Delaware lost 14.1 percent of its teachers and nearly one-third of its students from its public elementary and secondary schools from 1972-73 to 1982-83. New York similarly dropped from 186,943 teachers in 1972-73 to an

TABLE 14. Numbers of classroom teachers in public elementary and secondary schools and percentage change, by state: 1972-73 and 1982-83

State	1972-73	1982-83	Percentage Change
United States	2,108,846	2,138,572	1.4
Alabama	34,234	39,400	15.0
Alaska	4,142	5,630	35.9
Arizona	21,403	28,856	34.8
Arkansas	20,611	23,505	14.0
California	187,552	170,397	-9.1
Colorado	24,879	29,000	16.6
Connecticut	34,168	31,698	-7.2
Delaware	6,220	5,344	-14.1
District of Columbia	6,530	4,909	-24.8
Florida	66,787	82,041	22.8
Georgia	49,091	57,016	16.1
Hawaii	6,968	8,124	16.6
Idaho	8,112	10,125	24.8
Illinois	109,823	104,249	-5.1
Indiana	52,318	50,692	-3.1
Iowa	30,940	31,013	0.2
Kansas	25,739	26,280	2.1
Kentucky	31,417	32,200	2.5
Louisiana	40,009	42,499	6.2
Maine	11,246	12,277	9.2
Maryland	42,327	37,746	-10.8
Massachusetts	57,531	52,00	-9.6
Michigan	90,218	77,206	-14.4
Minnesota	45,455	40,643	-10.6
Mississippi	23,429	24,842	6.0
Missouri	47,027	48,257	2.6
Montana	8,500	8,906	4.8
Nebraska	17,579	16,249	-7.6
Nevada	5,411	7,442	37.5
New Hampshire	8,313	10,105	21.6
New Jersey	77,561	73,291	-5.5
New Mexico	12,190	14,250	16.9
New York	186,943	163,100	-12.8
North Carolina	50,033	56,459	12.8
North Dakota	7,160	7,499	4.7
Ohio	104,624	95,010	-9.2
Oklahoma	28,192	33,900	20.2
Oregon	22,125	24,500	10.7
Pennsylvania	111,682	102,700	-8.0
Rhode Island	9,490	8,758	-7.7
South Carolina	26,915	32,080	19.2
South Dakota	8,161	7,974	-2.3
Tennessee	37,142	39,233	5.6
Texas	130,517	166,800	27.8
Utah	12,320	14,889	20.8
Vermont	6,030	6,591	9.3
Virginia	53,606	56,892	6.1
Washington	32,725	34,497	5.4
West Virginia	17,817	22,001	23.5
Wisconsin	51,142	52,200	2.1
Wyoming	4,492	7,297	62.4

SOURCE: Computed from selected data in The National Education Association, Estimates of School Statistics: 1973-74, (Washington: National Education Association, 1974), p. 28; and Estimates of School Statistics: 1982-83, (Washington: National Education Association, January 1983), p. 34.

TABLE 15. Average number of students per teacher, by state: 1972-73 and 1982-83

	Elementary and Secondary Schools		Elementary Schools		Secondary Schools	
	1972-73	1982-83	1972-73	1982-83	1972-73	1982-83
United States	22	18	23	20	20	16
Alabama	23	18	24	19	22	17
Alaska	20	15	22	16	18	15
Arizona	24	19	25	19	24	18
Arkansas	22	19	24	20	20	17
California	24	23	24	26	24	19
Colorado	23	19	25	21	21	17
Connecticut	20	16	25	18	13	13
Delaware	22	17	26	19	18	16
District of Columbia	21	18	22	17	20	19
Florida	25	18	26	17	23	19
Georgia	22	18	28	19	20	18
Hawaii	26	20	24	17	28	24
Idaho	23	20	24	22	21	18
Illinois	21	18	23	19	19	16
Indiana	23	20	25	21	22	19
Iowa	21	16	23	18	18	14
Kansas	19	15	21	17	17	14
Kentucky	23	20	23	21	22	20
Louisiana	21	18	24	23	18	12
Maine	22	17	26	19	16	14
Maryland	22	19	24	19	20	18
Massachusetts	21	18	23	28	18	10
Michigan	24	23	24	23	24	23
Minnesota	20	18	22	18	18	17
Mississippi	23	19	23	18	22	18
Missouri	22	17	30	23	13	10
Montana	20	17	23	22	16	11
Nebraska	19	16	19	18	18	14
Nevada	24	20	25	21	24	20
New Hampshire	20	16	22	18	18	14
New Jersey	19	16	23	17	15	14
New Mexico	23	19	22	22	24	16
New York	19	17	20	18	17	16
North Carolina	23	20	24	23	21	15
North Dakota	20	16	21	17	18	13
Ohio	23	20	26	21	19	18
Oklahoma	22	17	22	19	21	16
Oregon	22	18	23	18	20	18
Pennsylvania	21	17	23	19	20	16
Rhode Island	20	16	21	15	19	17
South Carolina	23	19	24	21	22	15
South Dakota	20	16	21	16	18	14
Tennessee	24	21	25	24	23	16
Texas	22	18	22	21	21	14
Utah	25	25	26	24	24	25
Vermont	18	14	20	16	14	12
Virginia	20	17	22	18	17	16
Washington	24	21	22	21	27	22
West Virginia	23	17	24	18	22	16
Wisconsin	20	15	21	15	18	14
Wyoming	19	14	20	15	18	13

SOURCE: Computed from selected data in The National Education Association, Estimates of School Statistics: 1973-74, (Washington: National Education Association, 1974), pp. 25, 28; and Estimates of School Statistics: 1982-83, (Washington: National Education Association, January 1983), pp. 30, 34.

TABLE 16. States with greatest losses in enrollment and in numbers of classroom Teachers, ranked: 1972–73 to 1982–83

State	Percentage Change in Number of Teachers from 1972-73 to 1982-83	Percentage Change in Enrollment from 1972-73 to 1982-83	Number of Students per Teacher	
			1972-73	1982-83
1. District of Columbia	-24.8	-37.4	21	18
2. Michigan	-14.4	-19.7	24	23
3. Delaware	-14.1	-31.0	22	17
4. New York	-12.8	-22.9	19	17
5. Maryland	-10.8	-24.1	22	19
6. Minnesota	-10.6	-21.0	20	18
7. Massachusetts	-9.6	-23.0	21	18
8. Ohio	-9.2	-23.4	23	20
9. California	-9.1	-12.0	24	23
10. Pennsylvania	-8.0	-24.6	21	17
11. Rhode Island	-7.7	-27.5	20	16
12. Nebraska	-7.6	-19.6	19	16
13. Connecticut	-7.2	-25.0	20	16
14. New Jersey	-5.5	-22.8	19	16
15. Illinois	-5.1	-20.3	21	18
16. Indiana	-3.1	-17.6	23	20
17. South Dakota	-2.3	-23.8	20	16

SOURCE: Selected data from The National Education Association, Estimates of School Statistics: 1973-74, (Washington: National Education Association, 1974), pp. 25, 28; and Estimates of School Statistics: 1982-83, (Washington: National Education Association, January 1983), pp. 30, 34.

estimated 163,100 (12.8 percent) in 1982-83 while its school enrollment declined from 3,494,805 to 2,693,000 (22.9 percent). Maryland's number of teachers dropped 10.8 percent and its number of students 24.1 percent. Minnesota lost 10.6 percent of its teachers and 21.0 percent of its students; Massachusetts, 9.6 percent and 23.0 percent; Ohio, 9.2 percent and 23.4 percent; California, 9.1 percent and 12.0 percent; Pennsylvania 8.0 percent and 24.6 percent; Rhode Island, 7.7 percent and 27.5 percent; Nebraska, 7.6 percent and 19.6 percent; Connecticut, 7.2 percent and 25.0 percent; New Jersey, 5.5 percent and 22.8 percent; Illinois, 5.1 percent and 20.3 percent; Indiana, 3.1 percent and 17.6 percent; and South Dakota, 2.3 percent and 23.8 percent.

Thirty-two states added to their totals of teachers in public elementary and secondary schools even though only seven of them had an increase in total elementary and secondary school enrollment from 1972-73 to 1982-83. All seven are in the West (Table 17).

Public Secondary School Teachers

Overall, the number of teachers in public secondary schools in the United States decreased by less than 1 percent, from 965,908 in 1972-73 to 961,861 in 1982-83. Over one-third of the states (18) and the District of Columbia had fewer teachers in their public secondary schools in 1982-83 than a decade earlier. These states also showed significant declines in their statewide secondary school student enrollment. Three-fourths of these states are located in the Northeast and North Central regions (Tables 18 and 19).

Only six states--all in the West except one (Vermont)--registered increases in public secondary school enrollments in the past decade, whereas 31 states showed an overall increase in the number of secondary school teachers.

In Nevada, public secondary school enrollment went from 58,917 in 1972-73 to an estimated 69,460 in 1982-83, a 17.9 percent increase. In the same period, Nevada raised the number of its secondary teachers by 40.7 percent, from 2,505 to an estimated 3,525.

Arizona increased its number of secondary teachers 41.5 percent, from 6,322 to an estimated 8,947, while increasing secondary enrollment by 10.1 percent (from

TABLE 17. States that added classroom teachers with corresponding percentage change in enrollment, ranked: 1972-73 to 1982-83

	State	Percentage Change in Number of Teachers from 1972-73 to 1982-83	Percentage Change in Enrollment from 1972-73 to 1982-83	Number of Students per Teacher 1972-73	1982-83
	United States	1.4	-14.0	22	18
1.	Wyoming	62.4	18.9	19	14
2.	Nevada	37.5	14.7	24	20
3.	Alaska	35.9	2.4	20	15
4.	Arizona	34.8	4.4	24	19
5.	Texas	27.8	5.3	22	18
6.	Idaho	24.8	11.0	23	20
7.	West Virginia	23.5	-8.5	23	17
8.	Florida	22.8	-10.4	25	18
9.	Utah	20.8	20.7	25	25
10.	Oklahoma	20.2	-4.3	22	17
11.	South Carolina	19.2	-3.1	23	19
12.	New Mexico	16.9	-4.1	23	19
13.	Colorado	16.6	-5.1	23	19
14.	Hawaii	16.6	-9.0	26	20
15.	Georgia	16.1	-3.6	22	18
16.	Alabama	15.0	-7.6	23	18
17.	Arkansas	14.0	-4.5	22	19
18.	North Carolina	12.8	-4.7	23	20
19.	Oregon	10.7	-6.3	22	18
20.	Vermont	9.3	-14.0	18	14
21.	Louisiana	6.2	-8.5	21	18
22.	Virginia	6.1	-8.8	20	17
23.	Mississippi	6.0	-12.4	23	19
24.	Tennessee	5.6	-6.3	24	21
25.	Washington	5.4	-6.6	24	21
26.	Montana	4.8	-11.7	20	17
27.	North Dakota	4.7	-17.6	20	16
28.	Missouri	2.6	-21.7	22	17
29.	Kentucky	2.5	-8.8	23	20
30.	Wisconsin	2.1	-21.1	20	15
31.	Kansas	2.1	-17.4	19	15
32.	Iowa	0.2	-23.2	21	16

SOURCE: Computed from selected data in The National Education Association, Estimates of School Statistics: 1973-74, (Washington: National Education Association, 1974), pp. 25, 28; and Estimates of School Statistics: 1982-83, (Washington: National Education Association, January 1983), pp. 30, 34.

TABLE 18. Numbers of teachers in public secondary schools, percentages who are women and percentage change in total, by state: 1972-73 and 1982-83

State	Secondary Teachers 1972-73	Percentage Who Are Women	Secondary Teachers 1982-83	Percentage Who Are Women	Percentage Change in Total from 1972-73 to 1982-83
United States	965,908	46.4	961,861	49.3	-0.4
Alabama	17,288	60.8	19.449	62.0	12.5
Alaska	1,804	44.6	2,528	42.7	40.1
Arizona	6,322	38.8	8,947	41.3	41.5
Arkansas	10,603	53.0	11,964	60.5	12.8
California	74,275	30.9	65,757	45.9	-11.5
Colorado	12,489	44.0	13,978	43.6	11.9
Connecticut	14,825	45.0	12,608	46.2	-15.0
Delaware	3,484	43.9	2,856	46.5	-18.0
District of Columbia	2,724	63.8	2,012	64.6	-26.1
Florida	33,289	51.9	35,537	57.3	6.8
Georgia	19,565	39.9	22,276	56.5	13.8
Hawaii	2,926	44.6	3,137	56.5	7.2
Idaho	4,319	42.7	4,775	42.9	10.6
Illinois	46,426	40.2	36,444	48.4	22.3
Indiana	25,966	42.4	25,159	45.0	-3.1
Iowa	15,679	40.0	16,398	42.4	4.6
Kansas	12,746	43.5	11,780	44.3	-7.6
Kentucky	11,949	53.6	11,200	54.0	-0.6
Louisiana	18,503	58.2	18,716	58.3	1.2
Maine	4,473	36.7	4,499	36.0	0.6
Maryland	20,765	52.5	19,673	50.1	-5.2
Massachusetts	28,475	46.5	30,000	43.3	5.4
Michigan	41,125	48.7	37,107	49.0	-11.1
Minnesota	23,981	35.4	21,239	40.1	-11.4
Mississippi	10,257	56.0	11,178	62.0	9.0
Missouri	22,069	49.9	24,257	57.1	9.9
Montana	3,362	34.0	3,934	34.9	17.0
Nebraska	8,062	41.9	8,130	46.1	0.8
Nevada	2,505	39.9	3,525	41.1	40.7
New Hampshire	3,851	43.0	4,784	49.7	24.2
New Jersey	35,678	47.0	31,515	43.0	-11.7
New Mexico	5,772	45.6	7,320	50.5	26.8
New York	95,752	46.1	89,300	44.1	-6.7
North Carolina	17,035	58.0	22,251	61.6	30.6
North Dakota	2,601	33.6	2,780	38.1	6.9
Ohio	48,579	44.3	41,630	43.5	-14.3
Oklahoma	13,250	47.9	16,000	53.8	20.8
Oregon	9,937	37.2	9,500	36.8	-4.4
Pennsylvania	57,693	42.1	55,458	44.4	-3.9
Rhode Island	3,868	41.8	4,094	41.4	5.8
South Carolina	10,783	61.7	11,950	63.6	10.8
South Dakota	2,949	38.1	2,696	40.8	-8.6
Tennessee	14,973	56.4	14,752	55.2	-1.5
Texas	61,343	59.2	74,000	57.8	20.6
Utah	6,046	36.6	5,804	36.5	-4.0
Vermont	2,820	42.7	3,604	45.3	27.8
Virginia	23,120	59.2	23,218	63.1	0.4
Washington	14,094	37.5	16,116	37.8	14.3
West Virginia	8,205	53.6	9,288	54.0	13.2
Wisconsin	23,934	36.5	23,400	41.5	-2.2
Wyoming	2,269	35.8	3,338	46.3	47.1

SOURCE: Selected data from The National Education Association, Estimates of School Statistics: 1973-74, (Washington: National Education Association, 1974), p. 28; and Estimates of School Statistics: 1982-83, (Washington: National Education Association, January 1983), p. 34.

TABLE 19. States that had the greatest loss in numbers of secondary teachers with their percentage changes in numbers of elementary teachers and in secondary school enrollments, ranked: 1972-73 and 1982-83

	State	Percentage Change in Secondary Teachers	Percentage Change in Elementary Teachers	Percentage Change in Secondary Enrollment	Number of Secondary Students per Teacher 1972-73	Number of Secondary Students per Teacher 1982-83
1.	District of Columbia	-26.1	-23.9	-30.8	20	19
2.	Illinois	-22.3	7.8	-33.5	19	16
3.	Delaware	-18.0	-9.1	-28.0	19	16
4.	Connecticut	-15.0	-1.3	-13.8	13	13
5.	Ohio	-14.3	-4.8	-22.5	19	18
6.	New Jersey	-11.7	-0.2	-18.5	15	14
7.	California	-11.5	-7.6	-29.0	24	19
8.	Minnesota	-11.4	-9.6	-18.5	18	17
9.	Michigan	-11.1	-17.3	-17.6	24	23
10.	South Dakota	-8.6	1.3	-27.1	18	14
11.	Kansas	-7.6	11.6	-25.0	17	14
12.	New York	-6.7	-19.0	-14.4	17	14
13.	Maryland	-5.2	16.2	-13.6	20	18
14.	Oregon	-4.4	23.1	-13.4	20	18
15.	Pennsylvania	-3.9	-12.5	-20.7	20	16
16.	Indiana	-3.1	-3.1	-15.7	22	19
17.	Wisconsin	-2.2	5.8	-19.2	18	14
18.	Tennessee	-1.5	10.4	-30.1	23	16
19.	Kentucky	-0.6	7.9	-17.0	22	20

SOURCE: Computed from selected data in The National Education Association, Estimates of School Statistics: 1973-74, (Washington: National Education Association, 1974), pp. 25, 28; and Estimates of School Statistics: 1982-83, (Washington: National Education Association, January 1983), pp. 30, 34.

148,792 to 164,000) during that same period. Alaska, to accommodate increased enrollment and smaller class size, went from 1,804 secondary teachers to 2,538 (a 40.1 percent increase), and boosted secondary enrollment from 33,312 in 1972-73 to 38,014 in 1982-83 (14.1 percent).

Vermont raised its number of public secondary school teachers by 27.8 percent, from 2,820 in 1972-73 to an estimated 3,604 in 1982-83. Enrollment increased by only 5.7 percent, from 41,002 to 43,336.

Wyoming increased its number of secondary teachers by nearly 50 percent even though enrollment increased by only 5.6 percent, pushing the student to teacher ratio from 18:1 to 13:1 in the decade.

Utah's public secondary school enrollment increased slightly (4.0 percent) from 142,192 in 1972-73 to 147,817 in 198~-83, but Utah had fewer secondary teachers in 1982-83 (5,804) than it did a decade earlier (6,046). Utah's public secondary student-teacher ratio went from 24:1 to 25:1 in the ten years.

Five additional states increased their public secondary teaching staffs by more than 20 percent—North Carolina (30.6 percent), New Mexico (26.8 percent), New Hampshire (24.2 percent), Oklahoma (20.8 percent), and Texas (20.6 percent). Twenty-one others added some secondary teachers in the past decade.

More than one-third of the states—most in the Northeast and North Central regions—and District of Columbia lost secondary teachers in the past ten years. They also lost enrollment in their public secondary schools (Table 19).

Public Elementary School Teachers

Across the United States, the number of teachers in public elementary schools increased by 3.0 percent from 1972-73 to 1982-83. However, 17 states and the District of Columbia had a net decrease in the number of public elementary school teachers for that period. As with states that lost in numbers of secondary school teachers, those with a drop in the number of elementary teachers are in the country's Northeast and North Central regions (Table 20).

Seven Western and two Southern states showed more than a 30 percent increase in the number of public elementary school teachers from 1972-73 to 1982-83, and 24 other states had some increases. However, only ten states had an increase in enrollments in their public elementary schools.

Wyoming's public elementary teaching staff rose by 78.1 percent, from 2,223 to 3,959, in the past decade; its enrollment increased by 30.6 percent. Utah increased its number of public elementary teachers by 44.8 percent, from 6,274 to 9,085, and its enrollment from 163,724 to 221,521 (35.3 percent) in that period (Table 21).

Massachusetts had the largest percentage drop in total number of public elementary school teachers in the decade, from 29,056 in 1972-73 to an estimated 22,000 in 1982-83—almost one-fourth fewer. Massachusetts' public elementary school enrollment dropped 9.0 percent during the same period.

The student-teacher ratio for public elementary schools increased in only two states in the past decade—in Massachusetts from 23:1 to 28:1, and in California from 24:1 to 26:1. California voters adopted Proposition 13 in 1978 and Massachusetts voted in Proposition 2 $\frac{1}{2}$ in 1980. Both limited the amount that

TABLE 20. Numbers of teachers in public elementary schools, percentages who are women and percentage change in total, by state: 1972-73 and 1982-83

State	Elementary Teachers 1972-73	Percentage Who Are Women	Elementary Teachers 1982-83	Percentage Who Are Women	Percentage Change in Total from 1972-73 to 1982-83
50 States and D.C.	1,142,938	83.6	1,176,711	83.4	3.0
Alabama	16,946	90.9	19,951	94.1	17.7
Alaska	2,338	73.8	3,102	77.5	32.7
Arizona	15,081	73.7	19,909	76.2	32.0
Arkansas	10,008	92.0	11,541	94.7	15.3
California	113,277	78.0	104,640	76.5	-7.6
Colorado	12,390	82.5	15,022	80.7	21.2
Connecticut	19,343	75.0	19.090	76.5	-1.3
Delaware	2,736	83.4	2,488	85.0	-9.1
District of Columbia	3,806	89.8	2,897	88.4	-23.9
Florida	33,498	87.8	46,504	85.3	38.8
Georgia	29,526	91.4	34,740	91.7	17.6
Hawaii	4,042	91.5	4,987	91.1	23.4
Idaho	3,793	86.7	5,350	83.0	41.0
Illinois	62,897	76.6	67,805	78.8	7.8
Indiana	26,352	84.1	25,533	83.6	-3.1
Iowa	15,261	90.0	14,615	88.3	-4.2
Kansas	12,993	88.5	14,500	88.9	11.6
Kentucky	19,468	82.9	21,000	83.0	7.9
Louisiana	21,506	88.6	23,783	90.4	10.6
Maine	6,773	76.2	7,778	74.7	14.8
Maryland	21,562	88.1	18,073	89.2	16.2
Massachusetts	29,056	84.2	22,000	82.6	-24.3
Michigan	48,493	86.0	40,044	86.0	-17.3
Minnesota	21,474	83.1	19,404	76.7	-9.6
Mississippi	13,172	90.8	13,664	92.0	3.7
Missouri	24,958	89.6	24,000	90.4	-3.8
Montana	5,138	80.9	4,972	77.5	-3.2
Nebraska	9,517	91.2	8,119	88.4	-14.7
Nevada	2,906	80.0	3,917	80.2	34.8
New Hampshire	4,462	85.0	5,321	83.1	19.2
New Jersey	41,883	79.0	41,776	78.0	0.2
New Mexico	6,418	84.5	6,930	85.1	8.0
New York	91,191	81.5	73,800	81.6	-19.0
North Carolina	32,998	85.0	34,208	88.4	3.7
North Dakota	4,559	76.8	4,719	81.4	3.5
Ohio	56,045	84.8	53,380	81.5	-4.8
Oklahoma	14,942	87.2	17,900	90.5	19.8
Oregon	12,188	75.7	15,000	73.0	23.1
Pennsylvania	53,989	80.2	47,242	76.1	-12.5
Rhode Island	5,622	81.4	4,664	81.2	-17.0
South Carolina	16,132	90.8	20,130	91.5	24.8
South Dakota	5,212	83.5	5,278	82.9	1.3
Tennessee	22,169	87.2	24,481	88.3	10.4
Texas	69,174	92.0	92,800	90.9	34.2
Utah	6,274	80.5	9,085	76.0	44.8
Vermont	3,210	78.3	2,987	84.8	-6.9
Virginia	30,426	88.6	33,674	89.1	10.4
Washington	18,631	73.7	18,381	71.6	-1.3
West Virginia	9,612	88.1	12,773	86.0	32.3
Wisconsin	27,208	79.0	28,800	74.3	5.8
Wyoming	2,223	83.4	3,959	84.7	78.1

SOURCE: Selected data from The National Education Association, Estimates of School Statistics: 1973-74, (Washington: National Education Association, 1974), p. 28; and Estimates of School Statistics: 1982-83, (Washington: National Education Association, January 1983), p. 34.

TABLE 21. States that added elementary classroom teachers with percentage change in elementary school enrollment, ranked: 1972-73 to 1982-83

State	Percentage Change in Elementary Teachers	Percentage Change in Elementary Enrollment	Student-Teacher Ratio 1972-73	Student-Teacher Ratio 1982-83
United States	3.0	-11.1	23	20
1. Wyoming	78.1	30.6	20	15
2. Utah	44.8	35.3	26	24
3. Idaho	41.0	28.7	24	22
4. Florida	38.8	-10.2	26	17
5. Nevada	34.8	12.2	25	21
6. Texas	34.2	23.3	22	21
7. Alaska	32.7	-5.3	22	16
8. West Virginia	32.2	-2.0	24	18
9. Arizona	32.0	2.2	25	19
10. South Carolina	24.8	8.9	24	21
11. Hawaii	23.4	-10.1	24	17
12. Oregon	23.1	-1.3	23	18
13. Colorado	21.2	-0.5	25	21
14. Oklahoma	19.8	-0.1	22	19
15. New Hampshire	19.2	-3.4	22	18
16. Alabama	17.7	-5.1	24	19
17. Georgia	17.6	-5.3	23	19
18. Maryland	16.2	-32.6	24	19
19. Arkansas	15.3	-1.7	24	20
20. Maine	14.8	-17.2	26	19
21. Kansas	11.6	-11.5	21	17
22. Louisiana	10.6	7.6	24	23
23. Tennessee	10.4	8.6	25	24
24. Virginia	10.4	-9.8	22	18
25. New Mexico	8.0	3.8	22	22
26. Kentucky	7.9	-3.9	23	21
27. Illinois	7.8	-12.5	23	19
28. Wisconsin	5.8	-22.6	21	15
29. Mississippi	3.7	-16.1	23	18
30. North Carolina	3.7	-3.6	24	23
31. North Dakota	3.5	-14.5	21	17
32. South Dakota	1.3	-22.3	21	16
33. New Jersey	0.2	-25.0	23	17

SOURCE: Computed from selected data in The National Education Association, Estimates of School Statistics: 1973-74, (Washington: National Education Association, 1974), pp. 25, 28; and Estimates of School Statistics: 1982-83, (Washington: National Education Association, January 1983), pp. 30, 34.

citizens could be taxed for such purposes as education. (For a more thorough treatment of this subject, see the section on public school finance, Page 50.)

The District of Columbia had a net loss of 23.9 percent of its public elementary school teachers in the decade. New York had an estimated 17,391 fewer teachers in its public elementary schools in 1982-83 than ten years earlier (a reduction of 19.0 percent), and enrollment in them dropped by nearly a third (from 1,878,260 to an estimated 1,308,600).

Michigan lost 17.3 percent of its teachers and 21.5 percent of its students in public elementary schools in the decade.

Thirteen additional states saw an overall decrease in the number of elementary public school teachers from 1972 73 to 1982-83 (Table 22).

Only nine states and the District of Columbia showed a drop in the number of both secondary public school teachers and elementary public school teachers, as well as in both elementary and secondary public school enrollments. With the exception of California, all of the states with such declines are in the industrialized North East and North Central regions.

Of all 50 states, Michigan was hit the hardest across-the-board, with declines in enrollments and numbers of teachers. New York lost the greatest proportion of students and teachers at the public elementary school level, followed by Pennsylvania. Delaware had the highest percentage decreases in numbers of students and teachers at the public secondary school level, just ahead of Connecticut and California (Table 23).

Composition of Teaching Force by Sex
Teaching in elementary and secondary schools in the United States, historically, has been a woman's trade. It still is. Of the teachers in public elementary schools, 83.6 percent were women in 1972-73, and it was virtually unchanged ten years later at 83.4 percent.

There is not much state-to-state variation in the ratios of women to men in either elementary or secondary schools. Southern states generally have the highest percentage of women teachers at both levels. Seven states in the South indicate

TABLE 22. States that decreased their numbers of elementary school teachers with percentage change in public elementary school enrollments, ranked: 1972–73 to 1982–83

State	Percentage Change in Elementary Teachers	Percentage Change in Elementary Enrollment	Student-Teacher Ratio 1972–73	Student-Teacher Ratio 1982–83
Massachusetts	−24.3	−9.0	23	28
District of Columbia	−23.9	−41.8	22	17
New York	−19.0	−30.3	20	18
Michigan	−17.3	−21.5	24	23
Rhode Island	−17.0	−40.8	21	15
Nebraska	−14.7	−16.8	19	18
Pennsylvania	−12.5	−28.2	23	19
Minnesota	−9.6	−23.8	22	18
Delaware	−9.1	−33.6	26	19
California	−7.6	−1.2	24	26
Vermont	−6.9	−26.3	20	16
Ohio	−4.8	−24.0	26	21
Iowa	−4.2	−26.4	23	18
Missouri	−3.8	−24.8	30	23
Montana	−3.2	−8.5	23	22
Indiana	−3.1	−19.3	25	21
Connecticut	−1.3	−29.5	25	18
Washington	−1.3	−7.6	22	21

SOURCE: Computed from selected data in The National Education Association, Estimates of School Statistics: 1973–74, (Washington: National Education Association, 1974), pp. 25, 28; and Estimates of School Statistics: 1982–83, (Washington: National Education Association, January 1983), pp. 30, 34.

more than 90 percent of their elementary teaching staffs are women, and more than 55 percent of those in secondary schools (Table 24).

State Variation in Racial and Ethnic Composition of Teaching Force

Southern states have the highest proportion of minority teachers, consistent with their higher proportion of minority students and overall minority population, as compared to states in other parts of the country (Table 25).

In 1980, of the fifty states, Mississippi had the highest proportion of minority teachers and students—38.6 percent for minority teachers and 51.6 percent for minority students. Louisiana followed with 35.3 percent and 43.4 percent, respectively. Then came Georgia, 27.6 percent and 34.3 percent; Alabama, 27.2 percent and 33.6 pecent; Florida, 26.7 percent and 32.2 percent; and South Carolina, 26.1 percent and 43.5 percent.

TABLE 23. States that had decreases in both their numbers of teachers and enrollments at the elementary and secondary levels: 1972–73 to 1982–83

State	Percentage Change in Elementary Enrollment	Percentage Change in Elementary Teachers	Percentage Change in Secondary Enrollment	Percentage Change in Secondary Teachers
District of Columbia	-41.8	-23.9	-30.8	-26.1
California	-1.2	-7.6	-29.0	-11.5
Connecticut	-29.5	-1.3	-13.8	-15.0
Delaware	-33.6	-9.1	-28.0	-18.0
Indiana	-19.3	-3.1	-15.7	-3.1
Michigan	-21.5	-17.3	-17.6	-11.1
Minnesota	-23.8	-9.6	-18.1	-11.4
New York	-30.3	-19.0	-14.4	-6.7
Ohio	-24.0	-4.8	-22.5	-14.3
Pennsylvania	-28.2	-12.5	-20.7	-3.9

SOURCE: Computed from selected data in The National Education Association, Estimates of School Statistics: 1973-74, (Washington: National Education Association, 1974), pp. 25, 28; and Estimates of School Statistics: 1982-83, (Washington: National Education Association, January 1983), pp. 30, 34.

TABLE 24. States with the highest proportion of women teachers in both elementary and secondary schools: 1972–73 and 1982–83

	Percentage of Women Teachers			
	Elementary Schools		Secondary Schools	
State	1972-73	1982-83	1972-73	1982-83
Alabama	90.9	94.1	60.8	62.0
Arkansas	92.0	94.7	53.0	60.5
Georgia	91.4	91.7	39.9	56.5
Hawaii	91.5	91.1	44.6	56.5
Mississippi	90.8	92.0	56.0	62.0
South Carolina	90.8	91.5	61.7	63.6
Texas	92.0	90.9	59.2	57.8

SOURCE: Selected data from The National Education Association, Estimates of School Statistics: 1973-74, (Washington: National Education Association, 1974), p. 28; and Estimates of School Statistics: 1982-83, (Washington: National Education Association, January 1983), p. 34.

TABLE 25. Percentages of minority enrollments and minority teachers, by state: Fall 1980

Region and State	Minority Enrollment as A Percentage of Total Enrollment K-12	Percentage of Minority Teachers
United States	26.7	12.5
New England		
Connecticut	17.0	5.7
Maine	0.9	0.2
Massachusetts	10.7	7.0
New Hampshire	1.3	0.4
Rhode Island	8.2	3.0
Vermont	1.0	0.3
Mid Atlantic		
Delaware	28.8	16.7
District of Columbia	96.4	NA
Maryland	33.5	23.5
New Jersey	28.4	NA
New York	32.0	7.8
Pennsylvania	14.9	7.1
Great Lakes		
Illinois	28.6	4.3
Indiana	12.0	6.4
Michigan	21.3	11.6
Ohio	14.7	6.9
Wisconsin	9.3	3.4
Plains		
Iowa	4.1	1.1
Kansas	12.7	4.9
Minnesota	5.9	0.8
Missouri	14.8	6.6
Nebraska	10.5	2.7
North Dakota	3.5	0.5
South Dakota	7.9	0.8
Southeast		
Alabama	33.6	27.2
Arkansas	23.5	16.5
Florida	32.2	26.7
Georgia	34.3	27.6
Kentucky	9.1	5.1
Louisiana	43.4	35.3
Mississippi	51.6	38.6
North Carolina	31.9	22.5
South Carolina	43.5	26.1
Tennessee	24.5	16.8
Virginia	27.5	19.1
West Virginia	4.3	3.0
Southwest		
Arizona	33.7	10.2
New Mexico	57.0	28.0
Oklahoma	20.8	12.3
Texas	45.9	26.9
Rocky Mountain		
Colorado	22.1	6.8
Idaho	8.2	1.6
Montana	12.1	2.3
Utah	7.3	2.5
Wyoming	7.5	2.4
Far West		
California	42.9	16.4
Nevada	18.9	9.8
Oregon	8.5	2.9
Washington	14.1	5.1
Alaska	28.4	7.3
Hawaii	75.2	NA

SOURCE: Computed by Feistrizer Publications, Washington, D.C.

CHAPTER III

Salaries of Classroom Teachers

The difference between the highest and lowest salary paid to a teacher in an elementary or secondary public school in the United States is nearly $20,000. Alaska's teachers drew $33,953, the highest average salary per year in 1982-83, while Mississippi's teachers earned the least at $14,285.

Two-thirds of the states paid their public elementary and secondary school teachers an average salary that was less than the estimated national average of $20,531 per year.

Such wide swings demand study and must be looked at in the context of numerous variables within each state: personal income levels for the state, per-capita income, population and school enrollment changes, total expenditures for public elementary and secondary schools, and expenditures per pupil in school (Chart 2).

Teacher Salaries State by State

There is wide variation among the states in salaries paid to public school teachers. Alaska's high average salary is nearly $9,000 more per year than the next highest, $25,100 in New York, and $10,000 more than Hawaii's $24,796 and Wyoming's $24,000.

In addition to Mississippi, other states with average salaries less than $17,000 per year include: South Carolina, $16,380; Arkansas, $15,176; Maine, $15,772; South Dakota, $15,595; New Hampshire, $14,353; and Vermont, $15,338.

Almost two-thirds of the states (31) pay their teachers less than the national average of $20,531. However, more than half of these states (18) raised their

44

CHART II.   State by state comparison of public elementary
             and secondary school teachers' salaries, 1972-73
             and 1982-83
SOURCE: Table 26

Elementary School Teachers   Secondary School Teachers

1972-73   1972-73
1982-83   1982-83

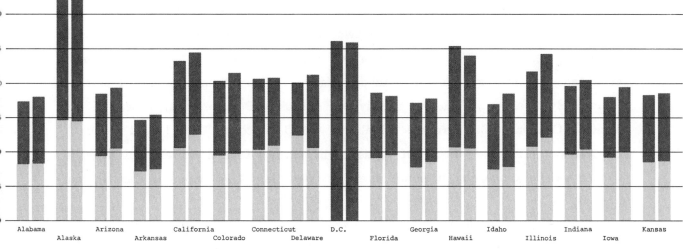

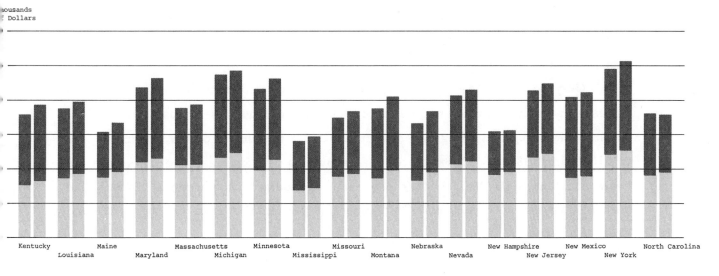

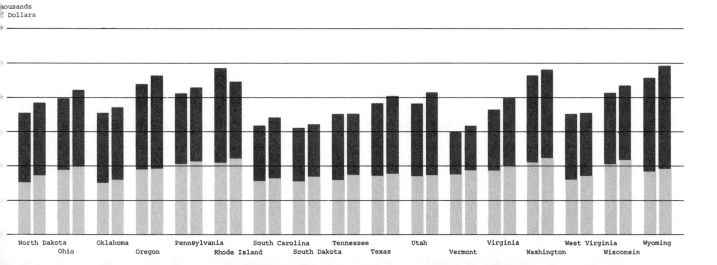

average teacher salaries by more than the national average (102 percent) in the past ten years. Altogether, 30 states exceeded the average increase nationwide and more than doubled teacher salaries in the last decade (Table 26).

States also varied considerably in how much they increased salaries of public elementary and secondary teachers over the past decade. Wyoming raised its average teacher salary by more than two-and-a-half times (158.2 percent) from $9,244 per year in 1972-73 to an estimated $24,000 in 1982-83. The next highest percentage increase in average teacher salary over the decade occurred in New Mexico (136.6 percent), followed closely by Kentucky (136.1 percent), Hawaii (135.4 percent), Oregon (132.6 percent), Oklahoma (132.1 percent), Utah (131.4 percent), and Alaska (131.3 percent). Of these eight states, four now have an average teacher salary above the national average (Wyoming, New Mexico, Hawaii, and Oregon).

When expressed in 1972 dollars, the average teacher salary actually dropped from $10,164 in 1972-73 to $8,926 in 1982-83, reflecting the loss of purchasing power due to inflation. Insofar as the consumer price index accurately measures cost-of-living increases, the real loss in the purchasing power of average teacher salaries totaled 12.2 percent over the past ten years.

Only seven states--six in the West and one in the South--showed a real increase in teacher salaries when 1982-83 (current) dollars were adjusted to 1972-73 dollars. Wyoming had the greatest increase (12.3 percent) from $9,294 in 1972-73 to $10,435 in 1982-83. Other states that showed a real increase over the same ten years included New Mexico (2.9 percent), Kentucky (2.6 percent), Hawaii (2.4 percent), Oregon (1.2 percent), Oklahoma (0.9 percent), Alaska (0.6 percent), and Utah (0.6 percent).

Four states--all in New England--recorded a loss in purchasing power in their average teacher salaries from 1972-73 to 1982-83: New Hampshire (from $9,157 in 1972-73 to $6,675 in 1982-83 dollars), a 27.1 percent loss of purchasing power; Vermont (from $8,887 to $6,669), a 25.0 percent loss; Maine ($8,976 to $6,857), a 23.4 percent loss; and Massachusetts ($10,520 to $8,261), a 21.5 percent loss).

Nineteen states and the District of Columbia paid teachers in their public elementary and secondary schools more, on the average, than the national average

TABLE 26. Average teachers' salaries, ranked by state, in 1982–83 current dollars and in adjusted 1972–73 dollars with percentage change from 1972–73 to 1982–83

State	Average Salary of Teachers in Current Dollars 1982-83	Percent of Increase Over 1981-82	1982-83 Average Salary in 1972-73 Dollars	Average Salary of Teachers in Current Dollars 1972-73	Percentage Change in Purchasing Power from 1972-73 to 1982-83
1. Alaska	$33,953	6.4	14,762	14,678	0.6
2. District of Columbia	26,048	7.3	11,325	NA	NA
3. New York	25,100	7.1	10,913	12,400	-12.0
4. Hawaii	24,796	10.0	10,781	10,533	2.4
5. Wyoming	24,000	12.9	10,435	9,294	12.3
6. Michigan	23,965	7.2	10,420	11,950	-12.8
7. California	23,555	3.5	10,241	12,072	-15.2
8. Washington	23,413	2.0	10,180	10,591	-3.9
9. Rhode Island	23,175	7.0	10,076	10,606	-5.0
10. Maryland	22,786	7.9	9,907	11,159	-11.2
11. Illinois	22,618	7.6	9,834	11,198	-12.2
12. Oregon	22,334	10.0	9,710	9,600	1.2
13. Minnesota	22,296	9.5	9,694	10,422	-7.0
14. New Jersey	21,642	8.7	9,410	11,730	-19.8
15. Colorado	21,500	9.8	9,348	9,666	-3.3
16. Pennsylvania	21,000	7.8	9,130	10,389	-12.1
17. Nevada	20,944	4.2	9,106	10,882	-16.3
18. Wisconsin	20,940	8.0	9,104	10,423	-12.6
19. Delaware	20,665	7.1	8,985	10,594	-15.2
20. New Mexico	20,600	10.2	8,956	8,705	2.9
50 States and D.C.	20,531	7.3	8,926	10,164	-12.2
21. Ohio	20,360	9.8	8,852	9,626	-8.0
22. Connecticut	20,300	7.5	8,826	10,600	-16.7
23. Indiana	20,067	7.8	8,725	10,048	-13.2
24. Utah	19,677	8.4	8,555	8,503	0.6
25. Texas	19,500	10.9	8,478	8,686	-2.4
26. Montana	19,463	9.5	8,462	8,908	-5.0
27. Louisiana	19,265	4.1	8,376	8,837	-5.2
28. Massachusetts	19,000	1.1	8,261	10,520	-21.5
29. Arizona	18,849	4.6	8,195	10,049	-18.4
30. Iowa	18,709	4.0	8,134	9,597	-15.2
31. Virginia	18,707	10.0	8,133	9,513	-15.5
32. Florida	18,538	10.5	8,060	9,276	-13.0
33. Kentucky	18,400	6.4	8,000	7,794	2.6
34. North Dakota	18,390	4.0	7,996	8,077	-1.0
35. Kansas	18,299	9.5	7,956	8,507	-6.5
36. Oklahoma	18,110	11.7	7,874	7,802	0.9
37. Alabama	17,850	14.4	7,761	8,105	-4.2
38. North Carolina	17,836	5.2	7,755	9,162	-15.4
39. Missouri	17,726	8.0	7,707	9,067	-15.0
40. Idaho	17,549	7.0	7,630	7,657	-0.4
41. Tennessee	17,425	7.0	7,576	8,300	-8.7
42. Georgia	17,412	6.4	7,570	8,204	-7.7
43. Nebraska	17,412	5.1	7,570	8,730	-13.3
44. West Virginia	17,370	1.4	7,552	8,119	-7.0
45. South Carolina	16,380	8.0	7,122	8,059	-11.6
46. Maine	15,772	4.4	6,857	8,976	-23.4
47. South Dakota	15,595	6.0	6,780	7,908	-14.2
48. New Hampshire	15,353	4.4	6,675	9,157	-27.1
49. Vermont	15,338	4.2	6,669	8,887	-25.0
50. Arkansas	15,176	4.6	6,598	7,325	-9.9
51. Mississippi	14,285	1.1	6,211	6,908	-10.1

SOURCE: Selected data from The National Education Association, Estimates of School Statistics: 1982–83, (Washington: National Education Association, January 1983), p. 35; and computations by Feistrizer Publications, Washington, D.C.

of $20,531 in 1982-83. But six of these states had salary increases over the past ten years that were below the national average of 102 percent—Michigan, 100.5 percent; California, 95.1 percent; New Jersey, 84.0 percent; Nevada, 92.5 per cent; Wisconsin, 100.9 percent; and Delaware, 95.1 percent. With the exception of California and Nevada, all of these states were hit hard by the recession. Neither Michigan, New Jersey, Wisconsin, nor Delaware increased its total personal income from 1972 to 1982 to any level close to the national average for increase in total personal incomes of 171 percent.

Salaries of Teachers in Elementary Schools and Secondary Schools Compared

Teachers in public secondary schools across the nation receive, on the average, higher salaries than teachers in public elementary schools (Table 27).

If this trend continues, it could mean cost savings for states in the next decade as population projections indicate declines in enrollments in secondary schools, which would mean less demand for teachers there. However, enrollments in elementary schools are expected to climb, as the baby boomlet of the late 1970s puts new pressures on elementary schools and their teachers.

The estimated average annual salary of a teacher in a public elementary school in the United States in 1982-83 was $20,042. This was $1,058 less per year than the average salary of $21,100 for secondary school teachers. Ten years ago, a secondary school teacher averaged $621 (6.3 percent) more per year than an elementary school teacher.

Still, four states—Florida, Hawaii, North Carolina, and Rhode Island—paid elementary school teachers slightly more than those in secondary schools.

In addition, over the past decade the average salary of public elementary school teachers rose slightly more than those of public secondary school teachers—102.9 percent compared to 101.0 percent. Twenty-nine states increased their salaries for elementary school teachers more, on the average, than they did those of public secondary teachers.

Analyses indicate that some states were determined to bring salaries of elementary school teachers more in line with those of secondary school teachers, which were perceived to be disproportionately higher a decade ago.

48

TABLE 27. Average salaries of public elementary school teachers and of public secondary school teachers with percentage changes, by state: 1972-73 and 1982-83

State	Average Salary of Classroom Teachers 1972-73		1982-83		Percentage Change	
	Elementary	Secondary	Elementary	Secondary	Elementary	Secondary
United States and D.C.	$ 9,876	$10,497	$20,042	$21,100	102.9	101.0
Alabama	8,024	8,184	17,400	18,000	116.8	121.4
Alaska	14,750	14,551	33,784	34,154	129.0	134.7
Arizona	9,500	10,600	18,637	19,318	96.2	82.2
Arkansas	7,209	7,450	14,789	15,548	105.1	108.7
California	11,668	12,688	23,240	24,538	99.2	93.4
Colorado	9,558	9,773	20,267	21,453	112.0	119.5
Connecticut	10,300	11,000	20,700	20,800	101.0	89.1
Delaware	12,443	10,710	20,062	21,166	92.1	97.6
District of Columbia	NA	NA	26,068	26,021	NA	NA
Florida	9,100	9,400	18,720	18,124	105.7	92.8
Georgia	7,916	8,613	17,111	17,847	116.2	107.2
Hawaii	10,634	10,389	25,335	24,024	138.2	131.2
Idaho	7,491	7,803	16,892	18,255	125.5	133.9
Illinois	10,743	12,143	21,747	24,242	102.4	99.6
Indiana	9,773	10,326	19,657	20,483	101.1	98.4
Iowa	9,146	10,035	17,978	19,361	96.7	92.9
Kansas	8,337	8,677	18,213	18,385	118.5	111.9
Kentucky	7,611	8,098	17,850	19,150	134.5	136.5
Louisiana	8,623	9,085	18,810	19,690	118.1	116.7
Maine	8,685	9,418	15,288	16,604	76.0	76.3
Maryland	10,910	11,417	21,780	23,142	99.6	102.7
Massachusetts	10,440	10,600	18,781	19,165	19.9	80.8
Michigan	11,600	12,200	23,732	24,217	104.6	98.5
Minnesota	9,819	11,211	21,450	23,068	118.5	105.8
Mississippi	6,757	7,102	14,049	14,571	107.9	105.2
Missouri	8,910	9,228	17,268	18,192	93.8	96.9
Montana	8,461	9,696	18,786	20,314	122.0	105.5
Nebraska	8,200	9,300	16,650	18,173	103.0	95.4
Nevada	10,721	11,030	20,585	21,306	92.0	93.2
New Hampshire	8,990	9,350	15,250	15,471	69.6	65.5
New Jersey	11,550	11,960	21,244	22,175	83.9	85.4
New Mexico	8,683	8,750	20,290	21,000	133.7	140.0
New York	12,000	12,700	24,300	25,700	102.5	102.4
North Carolina	8,929	9,373	17,847	17,754	99.9	89.4
North Dakota	7,715	8,644	17,680	19,110	129.2	121.1
Ohio	9,376	9,919	19,850	21,020	111.7	111.9
Oklahoma	7,601	8,012	17,660	18,600	132.3	132.2
Oregon	9,412	9,720	21,872	23,136	132.4	138.0
Pennsylvania	10,173	10,591	20,500	21,300	101.5	101.1
Rhode Island	10,286	11,071	24,070	22,154	134.0	100.1
South Carolina	7,890	8,175	15,890	17,040	101.4	108.4
South Dakota	7,638	8,253	15,386	15,988	101.4	93.7
Tennessee	8,020	8,710	17,369	17,517	116.6	101.1
Texas	8,589	8,784	19,000	20,100	121.2	128.8
Utah	8,369	8,633	19,078	20,615	128.0	138.8
Vermont	8,573	9,208	14,877	15,778	73.5	71.5
Virginia	9,209	9,913	18,020	19,655	95.7	98.3
Washington	10,320	10,950	22,977	23,923	124.6	118.5
West Virginia	7,866	8,372	17,290	17,479	119.8	108.8
Wisconsin	10,130	10,737	20,480	21,470	102.2	100.0
Wyoming	9,154	9,431	22,740	24,293	148.4	157.6

SOURCE: Selected data from The National Education Association, Estimates of School Statistics: 1973-74, (Washington: National Education Association, 1974), p. 30; and Estimates of School Statistics: 1982-1983, (Washington: National Education Association, January 1983), p. 35.

CHAPTER IV

Teachers and Schools in the Context of the Overall Economy

Salaries of classroom teachers comprised less than 38 percent of the total estimated expenditures for public elementary and secondary schools in 1982-83. The figure was 49 percent a decade ago. Total expenditures (including current expenditures, capital outlay, and interest) for 1982-83 were estimated by the National Education Association in January 1983 to be $116,931,093,000.[23] Salaries for elementary and secondary classroom teachers were an estimated $43,915,809,000 (computed by multiplying the estimated number of teachers, 2,138,572, by the average teacher salary, $20,531, which comes to 37.6 percent of the $116,931,093,000 total).

These total public elementary and secondary school expenditures rose by 126.3 percent in current dollars in the past decade, a decrease of 1.6 percent in real (1972) dollars from $51,673,393,000 in 1972-73 to $50,839,605,000 in 1982-83. Total personal income in the nation increased by 171 percent in current dollars from 1972 to 1982 but increased by only one-tenth that amount, or 17.8 percent in real (1972) dollars. By comparison, teachers salaries increased by only 102 percent in current dollars and actually decreased by 12.2 percent in real dollars over the same period (Chart 3).

Furthermore, total elementary and secondary school teachers' salaries, as a percentage of total personal income in the United States, dropped from a low of 2.7 percent in 1972 to an even lower 1.7 percent in 1982 (Table 28). Total expenditures for public elementary and secondary schools in the nation, as a percentage of total

CHART III. **State by state comparison of percentage change in average personal income and state expenditures for education between 1972-73 and 1982-83 relative to national averages. (In 1982, the national averge personal income was 170.9 higher than it was in 1972-73; in 1982, the national average for state school expenditures was 126.3 percent higher than it was in 1972-73).**

SOURCE: Table 32

  Personal Income   ■ Elementary/Secondary Public School Expenditures

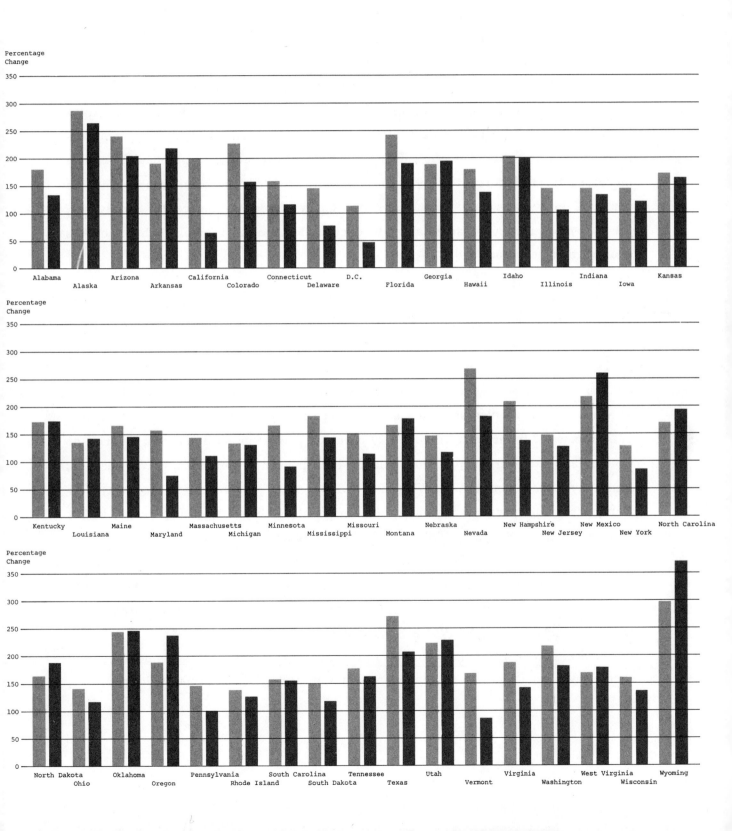

personal income, were 5.5 percent in 1972 and an estimated 4.6 percent in 1982 (Table 29).

Expenditures for public elementary and secondary education in the United States represented 3.6 percent of the Gross National Product in 1982,[24] about the same as it has been for the last fifteen years.

Per-capita income in the United States increased by nearly 145 percent in current dollars from 1972 to 1982, while per-pupil expenditure went up by 182 percent in current dollars during the same period. In real (1972) dollars, per-capita income increased by 6.5 percent in the past decade, while per-pupil expenditures rose by 22.5 percent. Per-pupil expenditure as a percentage of per-capita income increased from 23 percent in 1972 to 26 percent in 1982, and total personal income per pupil in average daily attendance shot up by almost 215 percent. Simply put, there is more money today relative to each child enrolled in public schools in this country than ten years ago.[25]

Teacher Salaries As Percentage of Total Elementary and Secondary School Expenditures

In 1982-83, Alabama spent by far the greatest proportion of its total public elementary and secondary school money, 60.5 percent, for classroom teachers' salaries. The next closest states all spent in the low 40 percent range: Missouri, 42.3; Texas, 42.0 percent; Illinois, 41.9 percent; Louisiana, 41.8 percent; District of Columbia, 41.8 percent; Rhode Island 41.6 percent; Nebraska, 41.2 percent; Kentucky, 41.2 percent; West Virginia, 41.1 percent; Wisconsin, 41.1 percent; New Hampshire, 40.8 percent; Wyoming, 40.4 percent; California, 40.0 percent; Idaho, 40.0 percent; and Virginia, 40.0 percent (Tables 30 and 31).

The state that put the smallest proportion of its total public elementary and secondary school expenditures into classroom-teacher salaries in 1982-83 was Michigan (29.0 percent). Alaska was the next lowest with 31.7 percent, although its average teacher pay of $33,953 is highest in the land.

Six states spent less than a third of their total public elementary and secondary school budgets on teacher salaries in 1982-83: Michigan (29.0 percent),

TABLE 28. Total spent on teachers' salaries as a percentage of personal income, by state: 1972 and 1982

State	1972	1982
United States	2.7	1.7
Alabama	2.3	2.1
Alaska	3.5	2.9
Arizona	2.5	1.9
Arkansas	2.3	1.9
California	2.2	1.3
Colorado	2.1	1.7
Connecticut	2.2	1.5
Delaware	2.2	1.5
District of Columbia	NA	1.4
Florida	1.9	1.3
Georgia	2.1	1.8
Hawaii	1.8	1.7
Idaho	2.1	2.0
Illinois	2.1	1.7
Indiana	2.3	1.8
Iowa	2.4	1.9
Kansas	2.1	1.7
Kentucky	2.0	1.8
Louisiana	2.7	1.9
Maine	2.6	1.9
Maryland	2.3	1.6
Massachusetts	2.1	1.4
Michigan	2.5	1.8
Minnesota	2.8	2.0
Mississippi	2.3	1.8
Missouri	2.1	1.7
Montana	2.6	2.2
Nebraska	2.3	1.7
Nevada	2.1	1.5
New Hampshire	2.3	1.5
New Jersey	2.3	1.6
New Mexico	2.7	2.4
New York	2.4	1.9
North Carolina	2.3	1.8
North Dakota	2.1	1.9
Ohio	2.1	1.7
Oklahoma	2.2	1.8
Oregon	2.2	2.0
Pennsylvania	2.2	1.7
Rhode Island	2.3	2.0
South Carolina	2.3	1.9
South Dakota	2.4	1.9
Tennessee	2.1	1.7
Texas	2.4	1.9
Utah	2.5	2.2
Vermont	2.9	2.1
Virginia	2.4	1.8
Washington	2.2	1.6
West Virginia	2.3	2.2
Wisconsin	2.7	2.2
Wyoming	2.7	2.9

SOURCE: Computed by Feistritzer Publications, Washington, D.C.

TABLE 29. Total public elementary and secondary school expenditures as a percentage of personal income, ranked by state: 1972 and 1982

	State	1982 Ranked	1972	Rank in 1972
1.	Alaska	9.0	9.6	1
2.	New Mexico	7.6	6.7	5
3.	Wyoming	7.2	6.1	12
4.	Utah	6.7	6.5	7
5.	Michigan	6.3	6.4	9
6.	Oregon	6.0	5.1	31
7.	Montana	5.8	5.6	20
8.	North Carolina	5.6	5.1	31
9.	Maine	5.5	5.9	13
10.	Vermont	5.5	7.8	3
11.	West Virginia	5.2	5.4	25
12.	Iowa	5.3	5.8	15
	North Dakota	5.3	5.1	31
	Wisconsin	5.3	5.8	15
15.	Minnesota	5.2	7.2	4
16.	Arkansas	5.1	4.6	47
	New York	5.1	6.3	10
18.	Arizona	5.0	5.5	22
	Idaho	5.0	5.0	35
	Mississippi	5.0	5.8	15
	South Carolina	5.0	5.7	19
22.	New Jersey	4.9	5.3	28
	Oklahoma	4.9	4.9	40
	Washington	4.9	5.5	22
25.	Delaware	4.8	6.5	7
	Indiana	4.8	5.0	35
27.	Georgia	4.7	4.6	47
	Kansas	4.7	4.8	42
	Rhode Island	4.7	5.0	35
	South Dakota	4.7	5.4	25
31.	Colorado	4.6	5.8	15
	Kentucky	4.6	4.4	50
	Pennsylvania	4.6	5.6	20
	United States	4.6	5.5	22
34.	Louisiana	4.5	6.2	11
	Maryland	4.5	6.6	6
	Texas	4.5	5.4	25
37.	Hawaii	4.4	5.2	30
	Ohio	4.4	4.9	40
	Tennessee	4.4	4.6	47
	Virginia	4.4	5.3	28
41.	Connecticut	4.3	5.1	31
	Massachusetts	4.3	5.0	35
43.	Nebraska	4.1	4.7	45
44.	Illinois	4.0	4.8	42
	Missouri	4.0	4.7	45
	Nevada	4.0	8.0	2
47.	Florida	3.7	4.3	51
	New Hampshire	3.7	4.8	42
49.	Alabama	3.4	4.1	52
	District of Columbia	3.4	5.0	35
51.	California	3.2	5.9	13

SOURCE: Computed from selected data in The National Education Association, Estimates of School Statistics: 1982-83, (Washington: National Education Association, January 1983), p. 39; U.S. Department of Commerce, Bureau of Economic Analysis, Commerce News, Report BEA #83-21, (Washington: U.S. Department of Commerce, May 1983), Table 3; The National Education Association, Estimates of School Statistics: 1973-74, (Washington: National Education Association, 1974), p. 34; and the U.S. Department of Commerce, Regional Economic Measurement Division, "State Personal Income, 1929-81: Revised Estimates", Survey of Current Business, (Washington: U.S. Government Printing Office, August 1982), p. 53.

TABLE 30. Teachers' salaries as a percentage of total public elementary/secondary school expenditures, by state: 1982-83

State	Number of Teachers	Average Salary	Total Spent on Teachers' Salaries (in thousands)	Total School Expenditures Including Capital Outlay and Interest (in thousands)	Teachers' Salary as Percentage of Total Expenses
50 States and D.C.	2,138,572	$20,531	$43,915,809	$116,931,093	37.6
Alabama	39,400	17,850	703,290	1,163,000	60.5
Alaska	5,630	33,953	191,155	602,174	31.7
Arizona	28,856	18,849	543,907	1,450,000	37.5
Arkansas	23,505	15,176	356,712	974,092	36.6
California	170,397	23,555	4,013,701	10,041,363	40.0
Colorado	29,000	21,500	623,500	1,643,730	37.9
Connecticut	31,698	20,300	643,469	1,851,303	34.8
Delaware	5,344	20,665	110,434	342,731	32.2
District of Columbia	4,909	26,048	127,870	306,258	41.8
Florida	82,041	18,538	1,520,876	4,175,000	36.4
Georgia	57,016	17,412	992,763	2,547,790	39.0
Hawaii	8,124	24,796	201,442	509,746	39.5
Idaho	10,125	17,549	177,684	445,650	40.0
Illinois	104,249	22,618	2,357,903	5,632,049	41.9
Indiana	50,692	20,067	1,017,236	2,656,179	38.3
Iowa	31,013	18,709	580,222	1,636,128	35.5
Kansas	26,280	18,299	480,898	1,296,812	37.1
Kentucky	32,200	18,400	592,480	1,437,400	41.2
Louisiana	42,499	19,265	818,743	1,959,920	41.8
Maine	12,277	15,772	193,633	560,494	34.5
Maryland	37,746	22,786	860,080	2,350,020	36.6
Massachusetts	52,000	19,000	988,000	2,993,931	33.0
Michigan	77,206	23,965	1,850,242	6,379,763	29.0
Minnesota	40,643	22,096	906,176	2,361,000	38.4
Mississippi	24,842	14,285	354,868	991,333	35.8
Missouri	48,257	17,726	855,404	2,019,991	42.3
Montana	8,906	19,463	173,337	454,552	38.1
Nebraska	16,249	17,412	282,928	686,242	41.2
Nevada	7,442	20,944	155,865	409,128	38.2
New Hampshire	10,105	15,353	155,142	380,000	40.8
New Jersey	73,291	21,642	1,586,164	4,745,380	33.4
New Mexico	14,250	20,600	293,550	935,200	31.4
New York	163,100	25,100	4,093,810	11,196,000	36.6
North Carolina	56,459	17,836	1,007,003	3,021,180	33.3
North Dakota	7,499	18,390	137,907	383,480	36.0
Ohio	95,010	20,360	1,934,404	5,137,700	37.7
Oklahoma	33,900	18,110	613,929	1,690,901	36.3
Oregon	24,500	22,334	547,183	1,645,070	33.3
Pennsylvania	102,700	21,000	2,156,700	5,932,400	36.4
Rhode Island	8,758	23,175	202,967	488,008	41.6
South Carolina	32,080	16,380	525,470	1,367,898	38.4
South Dakota	7,974	15,595	124,355	310,300	40.1
Tennessee	39,233	17,425	683,635	1,810,231	37.8
Texas	166,800	19,500	3,252,600	7,752,534	42.0
Utah	14,889	19,677	292,971	903,573	32.4
Vermont	6,591	15,338	101,093	266,936	37.9
Virginia	56,892	18,707	1,064,279	2,662,000	40.0
Washington	34,497	23,413	807,678	2,400995	33.6
West Virginia	22,001	17,370	382,157	930,797	41.1
Wisconsin	52,200	20,940	1,093,068	2,659,131	41.1
Wyoming	7,297	24,000	17,512	433,000	40.4

SOURCE: Selected data from The National Education Association, <u>Estimates of School Statistics: 1982-83</u>, (Washington: National Education Association, January 1983), pp. 34, 35, 39.

TABLE 31. Teachers' salaries as a percentage of total public elementary and secondary school expenditures, by state: 1972-73

State	Number of Teachers	Average Salary	Total Spent on Teachers' Salaries (in thousands)	Total School Expenditures Including Capital Outlay and Interest (in thousands)	Teachers' Salary as Percentage of Total Expenses
50 States and D.C.	2,108,846	$10,164	$21,435,876	$5,173,393	41.5
Alabama	34,234	8,105	277,467	497,429	55.8
Alaska	4,142	14,678	60,796	165,333	36.8
Arizona	21,403	10,049	215,079	475,820	45.2
Arkansas	20,611	7,325	150,976	306,449	49.3
California	187,552	12,072	2,264,128	6,104,621	37.1
Colorado	24,879	9,666	240,480	637,816	37.7
Connecticut	34,168	10,600	362,181	852,500	42.5
Delaware	6,220	10,594	65,895	192,830	34.2
District of Columbia	6,530	NA	NA	210,433	
Florida	66,787	9,276	619,516	1,445,033	42.9
Georgia	49,091	8,204	402,743	870,134	46.3
Hawaii	6,968	10,533	73,394	216,282	33.9
Idaho	8,112	7,567	62,114	149,620	41.5
Illinois	109,823	11,198	1,229,798	2,753,033	44.7
Indiana	52,318	10,048	525,691	1,146,179	45.9
Iowa	30,940	9,597	296,931	735,635	40.4
Kansas	25,739	8,507	218,962	494,734	44.3
Kentucky	31,417	7,794	244,864	521,987	46.9
Louisiana	40,0009	8,837	353,560	809,027	43.7
Maine	11,246	8,976	100,944	226,800	44.5
Maryland	42,327	11,159	472,327	1,341,439	35.2
Massachusetts	57,531	10,520	605,226	1,415,500	42.8
Michigan	90,218	11,950	1,078,105	2,761,000	39.0
Minnesota	45,455	10,422	1,073,732	1,229,500	38.5
Mississippi	23,429	6,908	161,848	407,522	39.7
Missouri	47,027	9,067	426,394	945,852	45.1
Montana	8,500	8,908	75,718	163,417	46.3
Nebraska	17,579	8,730	153,465	316,500	48.5
Nevada	5,411	10,882	58,883	145,600	40.4
New Hampshire	8,313	9,157	76,122	159,172	47.8
New Jersey	77,561	11,730	909,791	2,102,000	43.3
New Mexico	12,190	8,705	106,114	259,487	40.9
New York	186,943	12,400	2,318,093	6,073,100	38.2
North Carolina	50,033	9,162	458,402	1,031,359	44.4
North Dakota	7,160	8,077	57,831	133,300	43.4
Ohio	104,624	9,626	1,007,111	2,366,555	42.6
Oklahoma	28,192	7,802	219,954	487,400	45.1
Oregon	22,125	9,600	212,400	485,750	43.7
Pennsylvania	111,682	10,389	1,160,264	2,974,092	39.0
Rhode Island	9,490	10,606	100,651	215,036	46.8
South Carolina	26,915	8,059	216,908	537,445	40.4
South Dakota	8,161	7,908	64,537	143,006	45.1
Tennessee	31,142	8,300	308,279	694,350	44.4
Texas	130,517	8,686	1,133,671	2,524,761	44.9
Utah	12,320	8,503	104,757	275,458	38.0
Vermont	6,030	8,887	53,589	143,670	37.3
Virginia	53,606	9,513	509,954	1,110,011	45.9
Washington	32,725	10,591	346,590	857,417	40.4
West Virginia	17,817	8,119	144,656	336,003	43.1
Wisconsin	51,142	10,423	533,053	1,133,767	47.0
Wyoming	4,492	9,294	41,749	92,229	45.3

SOURCE: Computed from selected data in the National Education Association, Estimates of School Statistics: 1973-74, (Washington: National Education Association, 1974), pp. 28, 30, 34.

New Mexico (31.4 percent), Alaska (31.7 percent), Delaware (32.2 percent), Utah (32.4 percent), and Massachusetts (33.0 percent).

Personal Income and Total Public Elementary and Secondary School Expenditures State by State

Even though total expenditures for public elementary and secondary schools increased by 126 percent in current dollars across the United States in the past decade, nine states--all in the South and West--raised total school expenditures by more than 200 percent (Table 32). Wyoming led with the largest increase in total expenditures of nearly 370 percent. Wyoming's total personal income rose a whopping 294 percent in the same period, compared to the average national increase of 171 percent. The eight states following Wyoming included, in order, Alaska, New Mexico, Oklahoma, Oregon, Utah, Arkansas, Texas and Arizona (Table 33).

Thirteen states, all located in the Northeast and North Central regions, and the District of Columbia registered below the national average on both increases in total money spent for public elementary and secondary schools and in total personal income from 1972 to 1982.

California showed an increase in total school expenditures of 64.5 percent-- one-half the national average, but an increase in total personal income of 197.6 percent--well above the national average. While California's total population increased 20.1 percent, its public school enrollment decreased 12.0 percent during the last decade.

Behind the District of Columbia and California came Maryland, New York, and Vermont with the smallest increases in overall public elementary and secondary school expenditures in the past decade--75.2 percent, 84.4 percent, and 85.8 percent, respectively.

In real dollars, these states actually decreased their total school expenditures rather dramatically in the decade--Maryland by 23.8 percent, New York by 19.8 percent, and Vermont by 19.2 percent. All had significant declines in enrollment.

New York is the only state to show a loss in real personal income in the past

TABLE 32. Total personal income and total elementary/secondary public school expenditures in current and in adjusted 1972 dollars with percentage changes, by state: 1972-73 and 1982-83

	Personal Income 1972	Personal Income 1982	Percentage Change	School Expenditures 1972	School Expenditures 1982	Percentage Change	Total 1982 Personal Income in 1972 Dollars	Percentage Change in Actual Personal Income (1972 Dollars) Adjusted 1982 Dollars	Total 1982 School Expenditures in 1972 Dollars	School Expenditure Percentage Change
United States	944,852	2,559,904	170.9%	51,678,393	116,931,093	126.3	1,113,002	17.8	50,839,605	-1.6
New England										
Connecticut	16,773	43,158	157.3	852,500	1,851,303	117.2	18,764	11.9	804,914	-5.6
Maine	3,836	10,238	166.9	226,800	560,494	147.1	4,451	16.0	243,693	7.4
Massachusetts	28,502	68,913	141.8	1,415,500	2,993,931	111.4	29,962	5.1	1,301,709	-8.0
New Hampshire	3,328	10,184	206.0	159,172	380,000	138.7	4,428	33.0	165,217	3.8
Rhode Island	4,324	10,284	137.8	215,036	488,008	126.9	4,471	3.4	212,177	-1.3
Vermont	1,828	4,875	166.7	143,670	266,936	85.8	2,120	15.9	116,059	-19.2
Mid Atlantic										
Delaware	2,951	7,104	140.7	192,830	342,731	77.7	3,089	4.7	149,013	-22.7
District of Columbia	4,217	9,058	114.8	210,433	306,258	45.5	3,938	-6.6	133,156	-36.7
Maryland	20,215	52,011	157.3	1,341,439	2,350,020	75.2	22,613	11.9	1,021,748	-23.8
New Jersey	39,469	96,890	145.5	2,102,000	4,745,380	125.8	41,695	5.6	2,063,209	-1.8
New York	96,528	217,695	125.5	6,073,100	11,196,000	84.4	94,650	-1.9	4,867,826	-19.8
Pennsylvania	53,311	129,844	143.6	2,974,092	5,932,400	99.5	56,454	5.9	2,448,870	-17.7
Great Lakes										
Illinois	57,812	139,231	140.8	2,753,033	5,632,049	104.6	60,535	4.7	2,448,717	-11.0
Indiana	22,926	55,303	141.2	1,146,179	2,656,179	131.7	24,044	4.9	1,154,860	0.8
Michigan	43,282	100,668	132.6	2,761,000	6,379,763	131.1	43,769	1.1	2,773,810	0.5
Ohio	48,415	116,364	140.3	2,366,555	5,137,700	117.1	50,593	4.5	2,233,783	-5.6
Wisconsin	19,405	50,022	157.8	1,133,767	2,659,131	134.5	21,749	12.1	1,156,144	2.0
Plains										
Iowa	12,630	30,595	142.2	735,635	1,636,128	122.4	13,302	5.3	711,360	-3.3
Kansas	10,260	27,564	168.7	494,734	1,296,812	162.1	11,984	16.8	563,831	14.0
Minnesota	17,145	43,802	167.1	1,229,500	2,361,000	92.0	19,914	16.1	1,026,522	16.5
Missouri	20,159	50,374	149.9	945,852	2,019,991	113.6	21,902	8.6	878,257	-7.1
Nebraska	6,785	16,632	145.1	316,500	686,242	116.8	7,231	6.6	298,366	-5.7
North Dakota	2,745	7,200	162.3	133,300	383,480	187.7	3,130	1.4	166,730	25.0
South Dakota	2,637	6,564	148.9	143.006	310,300	117.0	2,854	8.2	134,913	-5.7
Southeast										
Alabama	12,117	33,833	179.2	497,429	1,163,000	133.8	14,710	21.4	505,652	1.7
Arkansas	6,596	19,093	189.5	306,449	974,092	217.9	8,301	25.8	423,518	38.2
Florida	33,345	113,273	239.7	1,445,033	4,175,000	188.9	49,249	47.7	1,815,217	25.6
Georgia	18,899	53,648	183.9	870,134	2,547,790	192.7	23,325	23.4	1,107,735	27.3
Kentucky	11,965	32,494	171.6	521,987	1,437,400	175.4	14,128	18.1	624,956	19.7
Louisiana	13,124	43,985	235.1	809,027	1,959,920	142.3	19,124	45.7	852,139	5.3
Mississippi	7,086	19,876	180.5	407,522	991,333	143.3	8,642	22.0	431,014	5.8
North Carolina	20,065	54,357	169.2	1,031,354	3,021,180	192.9	23,633	17.8	1,313,556	27.4
South Carolina	9,488	27,123	154.2	537,445	1,367,898	154.5	11,793	24.3	594,738	10.7
Tennessee	14,981	41,156	174.7	694,350	1,810,231	160.7	17,894	19.4	787,057	13.3
Virginia	21,112	60,422	186.2	1,110,011	2,662,600	139.9	26,270	24.4	1,157,653	4.3
West Virginia	6,428	17,249	168.3	336,003	930,797	177.0	7,500	16.7	404,694	20.4

	Personal Income 1972	Personal Income 1982	Percentage Change	School Expenditures 1972	School Expenditures 1982	Percentage Change	Total 1982 Personal Income in 1972 Dollars	Percentage Change in Actual Personal Income (1972 Dollars) Adjusted 1982 Dollars	Total 1982 School Expenditures in 1972 Dollars	School Expenditure Percentage Change
Southwest										
Arizona	8,609	29,180	238.9	475,820	1,450,000	204.7	12,687	47.4	630,435	32.5
New Mexico	3,873	12,230	215.8	259,487	935,200	260.4	5,317	37.3	406,609	56.7
Oklahoma	10,024	34,233	241.5	487,400	1,690,901	246.9	14,884	48.5	735,174	50.8
Texas	46,929	173,459	269.6	2,524,761	7,752,534	207.1	75,417	60.7	3,370,667	33.5
Rocky Mountain										
Colorado	10,998	35,853	226.0	637,816	1,643,730	157.7	15,588	41.7	714,655	12.0
Idaho	2,981	8,938	199.8	149,620	445,650	197.9	3,886	30.4	193,761	29.5
Montana	2,943	7,810	165.4	163,417	454,552	178.2	3,396	15.4	197,631	20.9
Utah	9,232	13,566	220.6	275,458	903,573	228.0	5,898	39.4	392,858	42.6
Wyoming	1,524	6,005	294.0	92,229	433,000	369.5	2,611	71.3	188,261	104.1
Far West										
California	104,191	310,097	197.6	6,104,621	10,041,363	64.5	134,825	29.4	4,365,810	-28.5
Nevada	2,815	10,348	267.6	145,600	409,128	181.0	4,499	59.8	177,882	22.2
Oregon	9,541	27,523	188.5	485,750	1,645,070	238.7	21,474	37.7	1,043,911	21.8
Washington	15,598	49,390	216.6	857,417	2,400,995	180.0	21,474	37.7	1,043,911	21.8
Alaska	1,726	6,655	285.6	165,333	602,174	264.2	2,893	67.6	261,815	58.4
Hawaii	4,178	11,530	176.0	216,282	509,746	135.7	5,013	20.0	221,629	24.7

SOURCE: Computed from selected data in the U.S. Department of Commerce, Regional Economic Measurement Division, "State Personal Income, 1929-81: Revised Estimates," Survey of Current Business, (Washington: U.S. Government Printing Office, August 1982), p. 53; U.S. Department of Commerce, Bureau of Economic Analysis, Commerce News, Report BEA #83-21, (Washington: U.S. Department of Commerce, May 1983), Table 3; The National Education Association, Estimates of School Statistics: 1973-74, (Washington: National Education Association, Estimates of School Statistics: 1982-83, (Washington: National Education Association, January 1983), p. 39.

TABLE 33.   States that had the greatest increases in total public school expenditures with their change in personal income: from 1972 to 1982

State	Percentage Change			
	Public School Expenditures		Personal Income	
	Current Dollars	Real (1972) Dollars	Current Dollars	Real Dollars
Wyoming	369.5	104.1	294.0	71.3
Alaska	264.2	58.4	285.6	67.6
New Mexico	260.4	56.7	215.8	37.3
Oklahoma	246.9	50.8	241.5	48.5
Oregon	238.7	47.2	188.5	25.4
Utah	228.0	42.6	220.6	39.4
Arkansas	217.9	38.2	189.5	25.8
Texas	207.1	33.5	269.6	60.7
Arizona	204.1	32.5	238.9	47.4

SOURCE: Computed from selected data in The National Education Association, Estimates of School Statistics: 1973-74, (Washington: National Education Association, 1974), p. 34; The National Education Association, Estimates of School Statistics: 1982-83, (Washington: National Education Association, January 1983), p. 39; the U.S. Department of Commerce, Regional Economic Measurement Division, "State Personal Income, 1929-81: Revised Estimates," Survey of Current Business, (Washington: U.S. Government Printing Office, August 1982), p. 53; and U.S. Department of Commerce, Bureau of Economic Analysis, Commerce News, Report BEA #83-21, (Washington: U.S. Department of Commerce, May 1983), Table 3.

decade--from $96,528,000,000 in 1972 to an adjusted $94,650,000,000 in 1982. New York's total population decreased by 3.8 percent in the decade.

However, it should be noted that New York was below only Alaska in spending per pupil in its public elementary and secondary schools in 1982-83, and it ranked fifth in per-capita income in 1982.

Per-Pupil Expenditures State by State

Probably the best simple indicator of a state's effort to support education is how much is spent on each pupil (Table 34). Per pupil expenditure in average daily attendance is computed by comparing total current expenditures with total number of pupils in average daily attendance (A⁻A) for the school year. The ADA formula is about 92 percent of fall enrollment across the country.

The per-pupil expenditure in 1982-83 was estimated at $2,917, up 182 percent in current dollars over the 1972-73 figure of $1,035. In adjusted 1972-73 dollars, the average per-pupil expenditure increased 22.5 percent from 1972-73 to 1982-83, whereas the average adjusted per-capita income increased 6.5 percent over the same period.

60

TABLE 34. Estimated current expenditures for public elementary and secondary schools per pupil in average daily attendance (ADA) in current dollars and in real (1972) dollars with percentage changes, ranked by state: 1972-73 and 1982-83

	State	Total 1982-83	Total 1972-73	Percentage Change	1982-83 amount in 72-73 dollars	Percentage change in real (1972) dollars
1.	Alaska	$6,620	$1,576	320.0	$2,878	82.6
2.	New York	4,302	1,649	160.9	1,870	13.4
3.	New Jersey	4,190	1,292	224.3	1,822	41.0
4.	Delaware	4,008	1,255	219.4	1,743	38.9
5.	Rhode Island	3,792	1,184	220.3	1,649	39.3
6.	District of Columbia	3,767	1,353	178.4	1,639	21.1
7.	Connecticut	3,746	1,241	201.9	1,629	31.3
8.	Michigan	3,648	1,159	214.8	1,586	36.8
9.	Oregon	3,643	1,015	258.9	1,584	56.1
10.	Maryland	3,486	1,188	193.4	1,516	27.6
11.	Wyoming	3,467	1,075	222.5	1,507	40.2
12.	Wisconsin	3,421	1,134	201.7	1,487	31.1
13.	Pennsylvania	3,290	1,165	182.4	1,430	22.7
14.	Hawaii	3,213	1,071	200.0	1,397	30.4
15.	Illinois	3,201	1,121	185.5	1,392	24.2
16.	Minnesota	3,157	1,160	172.2	1,373	18.4
17.	Iowa	3,147	1,057	197.7	1,368	29.4
18.	Kansas	3,094	933	231.6	1,345	44.2
19.	North Dakota	3,055	851	259.0	1,328	56.1
20.	Florida	3,009	941	219.8	1,308	39.0
21.	Colorado	2,986	1,002	198.0	1,298	29.5
22.	Montana	2,981	943	216.1	1,296	37.4
23.	Massachusetts	2,958	1,103	168.4	1,286	16.7
24.	Vermont	2,940	1,289	128.1	1,278	-0.9
	50 States and D.C.	2,917	1,035	181.8	1,268	22.5
25.	New Mexico	2,904	856	239.3	1,263	47.5
26.	Washington	2,887	933	191.2	1,255	34.5
27.	Ohio	2,807	954	194.2	1,220	27.9
28.	Oklahoma	2,792	768	263.5	1,214	58.1
29.	Virginia	2,740	941	191.2	1,191	26.6
30.	North Carolina	2,680	814	229.2	1,165	43.1
31.	Indiana	2,672	879	204.0	1,162	32.2
32.	Maine	2,651	844	214.1	1,152	36.5
33.	Nebraska	2,605	889	193.0	1,133	27.4
34.	Arizona	2,603	973	167.5	1,132	16.3
35.	Missouri	2,587	888	191.3	1,125	26.7
36.	Louisiana	2,529	928	172.5	1,100	18.5
37.	California	2,490	1,050	137.1	1,083	3.1
38.	West Virginia	2,480	811	205.8	1,078	32.9
39.	South Dakota	2,386	834	186.1	1,037	24.3
40.	Georgia	2,369	802	195.4	1,030	28.4
41.	New Hampshire	2,341	881	165.7	1,018	15.6
42.	Nevada	2,311	959	141.0	1,005	4.8
43.	Texas	2,299	840	173.7	1,000	19.0
44.	Kentucky	2,193	700	213.3	953	36.1
45.	Utah	2,128	761	179.6	925	21.6
46.	Tennessee	2,124	741	186.6	923	24.6
47.	Idaho	2,110	755	200.0	917	21.5
48.	Arkansas	2,093	658	218.0	910	38.3
49.	Mississippi	2,076	696	198.3	903	29.7
50.	South Carolina	2,016	799	152.3	877	9.8
51.	Alabama	1,546	599	158.1	672	12.2

SOURCE: Computed from selected data in The National Education Association, _Estimates of School Statistics: 1973-74_, (Washington: National Education Association, 1974), p. 34; and _Estimates of School Statistics: 1982-83_, (Washington: National Education Association, January 1983), p. 39.

Two-thirds of the states actually increased their expenditures per pupil in the past ten years above the national average of 182 percent. Alaska led with an increase of 320.0 percent in current dollars from $1,576 in 1972-73 to $6,620 in 1982-83. In adjusted 1972 dollars, Alaska's per-pupil expenditure increased 82.6 percent in the past decade. The next highest state was New York at $4,320 in 1982-83 up almost 161 percent in current dollars and 13.4 percent in real (1972) dollars over 1972-73. New Jersey followed at $4,190, up 224 percent in current dollars and 41.0 percent in real dollars above 1972-73. Delaware had the fourth highest ($4,008--219 percent higher in current dollars and 38.9 percent higher in real dollars from a decade earlier).

Alabama spent less per-pupil ($1,546) than any other state. However, Alabama increased its expenditures per pupil by almost 168 percent in the past ten years (still less than the national average of 182 percent) and devoted more of its total public elementary and secondary school expenditures to teacher salaries than any other state.

In real (1972) dollars, only one state, Vermont, showed a decrease in per-pupil expenditures, with almost a 1 percent drop (from $1,289 in 1972-73 to $1,278 in 1982-83).

Nearly one-third of the 50 states increased their per-pupil expenditures in real terms by more than a third of the 1972-73 amount.

Per-Capita Income State by State

Eight of the ten states that had the highest per-capita incomes in 1982 also ranked in the top 10 a decade earlier (Table 35). Alaska had the highest per-capita income in the nation in 1982 and the third highest in 1972, Connecticut was second in 1982 and 1972. California rose to fourth last year from ninth in 1972. New York was fifth in 1982 and fourth in 1972. Wyoming made the greatest leap, up from 23rd in 1972 to eighth in 1982. Texas went from 33rd in 1972 to 16th in 1982. Seventeen states overall had a per-capita income in 1982 above the national average of $11,056.

Per-capita income increased by more than the national average of 145

TABLE 35. Per capita income in current and real (1972) dollars with percentage chances, ranked by state: 1972 and 1982

	State	1982 Per Capita Income	Rank of Average Teacher's Salary	1972 Per Capita Income	1972 Rank	Percentage Change from 1972 to 1982	1982 Per Capita Income in 1972 Dollars	Percentage Change in Per Capita Income in Real (1972) Dollars
1.	Alaska	$15,200	1	$5,285	3	187.5	$6,609	25.1
2.	Connecticut	13,687	22	5,464	1	150.5	5,951	8.9
3.	New Jersey	13,027	14	5,380	2	142.1	5,664	5.3
4.	California	12,543	7	5,062	9	147.8	5,453	7.7
5.	New York	12,328	3	5,260	4	134.4	5,360	1.9
6.	Maryland	12,194	10	4,953	10	146.2	5,302	7.0
7.	Illinois	12,162	11	5,135	7	136.8	5,288	3.0
8.	Wyoming	11,970	5	4,395	23	172.4	5,204	18.4
9.	Massachusetts	11,921	28	4,946	11	141.0	5,183	4.8
10.	Delaware	11,796	19	5,143	6	129.4	5,129	-0.2
11.	Colorado	11,776	15	4,574	13	157.5	5,120	11.9
12.	Nevada	11,748	17	5,148	5	128.2	5,108	-0.8
13.	Washington	11,635	8	4,525	15	157.1	5,059	11.8
14.	Hawaii	11,602	4	5,107	8	127.1	5,043	-1.3
15.	Kansas	11,448	35	4,549	14	151.7	4,977	9.4
16.	Texas	11,352	25	3,991	33	184.4	4,936	23.7
17.	Minnesota	11,082	13	4,434	19	149.9	4,818	8.7
	United States	11,056		4,515		144.9	4,807	6.5
18.	Michigan	11,052	6	4,796	12	130.4	4,805	0.2
19.	Virginia	11,003	31	4,373	24	151.6	4,784	9.4
20.	Pennsylvania	10,943	16	4,478	17	144.4	4,758	6.3
21.	Florida	10,875	32	4,434	19	145.3	4,728	6.6
22.	Ohio	10,783	21	4,505	16	139.4	4,688	3.6
23.	Oklahoma	10,776	36	3,772	39	185.7	4,685	24.2
24.	North Dakota	10,746	34	4,351	25	147.0	4,672	7.4
25.	Rhode Island	10,730	9	4,429	21	142.3	4,665	5.3
26.	New Hampshire	10,710	48	4,258	30	151.5	4,657	9.4
27.	Iowa	10,532	30	4,415	22	138.6	4,579	3.7
28.	Wisconsin	10,497	18	4,314	28	143.3	4,564	5.8
29.	Nebraska	10,489	43	4,469	18	134.7	4,560	2.0
30.	Oregon	10,392	12	4,346	26	139.1	4,518	4.0
31.	Arizona	10,201	29	4,285	29	138.1	4,435	3.5
32.	Missouri	10,175	40	4,241	31	139.9	4,424	4.3
33.	Indiana	10,109	23	4,329	27	133.5	4,395	1.5
34.	Louisiana	10,083	27	3,489	47	189.0	4,384	25.7
35.	Montana	9,750	26	4,092	32	138.3	4,239	3.6
36.	Georgia	9,514	42	3,931	35	142.0	4,137	5.2
37.	South Dakota	9,506	47	3,893	37	144.2	4,133	6.2
38.	Vermont	9,446	49	3,947	34	139.3	4,107	4.1
39.	Idaho	9,259	39	3,906	36	137.0	4,026	3.1
40.	Maine	9,033	46	3,707	41	143.7	3,927	5.9
41.	North Carolina	9,032	38	3,789	38	138.4	3,927	3.6
42.	New Mexico	8,997	20	3,593	43	150.4	3,912	8.9
43.	Kentucky	8,861	33	3,586	44	147.1	3,853	7.4
44.	West Virginia	8,856	44	3,577	45	147.6	3,850	7.6
45.	Tennessee	8,849	41	3,664	42	141.5	3,847	5.0
46.	Utah	8,733	24	3,370	40	134.1	3,797	1.8
47.	Alabama	8,581	37	3,423	48	150.7	3,731	9.0
48.	South Carolina	8,468	45	3,490	46	142.6	3,682	5.5
49.	Arkansas	8,332	50	3,268	49	155.0	3,623	10.9
50.	Mississippi	7,792	51	3,071	50	153.7	3,388	10.3

SOURCE: Computed from selected data in the U.S. Department of Commerce, Regional Economic Measurement Division, "State Personal Income, 1929-81: Revised Estimates," Survey of Current Business, (Washington: U.S. Government Printing Office, August 1982), p. 57; and U.S. Department of Commerce, Bureau of Economic Analysis, Commerce News, Report BEA #83-21, (Washington: U.S. Department of Commerce, May 1983), Table 1.

percent in 20 states. However, seven of those 20 states still ranked among the bottom ten in per-capita income for 1982.

In real purchasing power (1972) dollars, Louisiana had the greatest increase in per-capita income (from $3,489 in 1972 to $4,384 in 1982—25.7 percent). Alaska followed with a 25.1 percent increase in adjusted 1972 dollars, trailed by Oklahoma, 24.2 percent; and Texas, 23.7 percent. All four states benefitted from being oil-rich in the past decade.

With the exception of North Carolina, the ten states in 1982 with the lowest per-capita incomes also were among the bottom ten in 1972. North Carolina was 41st in 1982 and 38th in 1972. Louisiana rose from 47th in 1972 to 34th in 1982.

In real dollars, per-capita income decreased slightly in three states from 1972 to 1982: Hawaii from $5,107 in 1972 to $5,043 in 1982 (down 1.3 percent); Nevada from $5,148 to $5,108 (down 0.8 percent); and Delaware from $5,143 to $5,129 (down 0.2 percent).

Per-Pupil Expenditures as Percentage of Per-Capita Income

Per-pupil expenditures as a percentage of per-capita income varied in 1982-83 from a high of 43.6 percent in Alaska to a low of 18.0 percent in Alabama (Table 36). The state with the second highest proportion of per-capita income relative to per-pupil expenditure was Rhode Island, 35.3 percent; followed by Oregon, 35.1 percent; New York, 34.9 percent, and Delaware 34.0 percent.

States other than Alabama having the smallest per-pupil expenditure as a percentage of per-capita income in 1982-83 included Nevada, 19.7 percent; California 19.9 percent; and Texas, 20.3 percent.

Total Personal Income Per Pupil in ADA

Another way to assess a state's available funds for education is to look at total personal income per pupil in average daily attendance. Total personal income in a state, divided by the total number of students in average daily attendence, should provide the amount available for school expenditures if all the state's personal income were spent on the students in public elementary and secondary schools—

TABLE 36. Per capita income, per pupil expenditures and per pupil expenditures as percentage of per capita income ranked by state, with percentage changes: 1972-73 and 1982-83

State	Per Capita Income		Expenditures Per Pupil in ADA		Per Pupil Expenditures as Percentage of Per Capita Income	
	1982	1972	1982-83	1972-73	1982 (ranked)	1972
Alaska	$15,200	$5,285	$6,620	$1,576	43.6	29.8
Rhode Island	10,730	4,429	3,792	1,184	35.3	26.7
Oregon	10,392	4,346	3,643	1,015	35.1	23.4
New York	12,328	5,260	4,302	1,649	34.9	31.3
Delaware	11,796	5,143	4,008	1,255	34.0	24.4
Michigan	11,052	4,796	3,648	1,159	33.0	NA
Wisconsin	10,497	4,314	3,421	1,134	32.6	24.8
New Mexico	8,997	3,593	2,904	856	32.3	23.8
New Jersey	13,027	5,380	4,190	1,292	32.2	24.0
Vermont	9,446	3,947	2,940	1,289	31.1	32.7
Montana	9,750	4,092	2,981	943	30.6	23.0
Pennsylvania	10,943	4,478	3,290	1,165	30.1	26.0
Iowa	10,532	4,415	3,147	1,057	29.9	22.7
North Carolina	9,032	3,789	2,680	814	29.7	21.5
Maine	9,033	3,707	2,651	844	29.3	22.8
Wyoming	11,970	4,395	3,467	1,075	29.0	24.5
Maryland	12,194	4,953	3,486	1,188	28.6	24.0
Minnesota	11,082	4,434	3,157	1,160	28.5	24.9
North Dakota	10,746	4,351	3,055	851	28.4	19.0
West Virginia	8,856	3,577	2,480	811	28.0	22.7
Florida	10,875	4,434	3,009	941	27.7	21.2
Hawaii	11,602	5,107	3,213	1,071	27.7	21.0
Connecticut	13,687	5,464	3,746	1,241	27.4	22.7
Kansas	11,448	4,549	3,094	933	27.0	19.4
Mississippi	7,792	3,071	2,076	696	26.6	22.7
Indiana	10,109	4,329	2,672	879	26.4	19.2
United States	11,056	4,515	2,917	1,035	26.4	22.9
District of Columbia	14,347	5,670	3,767	1,353	26.3	23.9
Illinois	12,162	5,135	3,201	1,121	26.3	20.2
Ohio	10,783	4,505	2,807	954	26.0	19.7
Arizona	10,201	4,285	2,603	973	25.5	22.7
Oklahoma	10,776	3,772	2,792	768	25.9	20.4
Missouri	10,175	4,241	2,587	888	25.4	19.8
Colorado	11,776	4,574	2,986	1,002	25.4	21.9
South Dakota	9,506	3,893	2,386	834	25.1	20.5
Arkansas	8,332	3,268	2,093	658	25.1	20.1
Louisiana	10,083	3,489	2,529	928	25.1	26.6
Georgia	9,514	3,931	2,369	802	24.9	20.4
Virginia	11,003	4,373	2,740	941	24.9	21.5
Massachusetts	11,921	4,946	2,958	1,102	24.8	22.3
Nebraska	10,489	4,469	2,605	889	24.8	19.0
Washington	11,635	4,525	2,887	933	24.8	20.6
Kentucky	8,861	3,586	2,193	700	24.7	19.5
Utah	8,733	3,730	2,128	761	24.4	20.4
Tennessee	8,849	3,664	2,124	741	24.0	20.2
South Carolina	8,468	3,490	2,016	799	23.8	20.7
Idaho	9,259	3,906	2,110	755	22.8	19.3
New Hampshire	10,710	4,258	2,341	881	21.9	20.7
Texas	11,352	3,991	2,299	840	20.3	21.0
California	12,543	5,062	2,490	1,050	19.9	20.7
Nevada	11,748	5,148	2,311	959	19.7	18.6
Alabama	8,581	3,423	1,546	599	18.0	17.5

SOURCE: Computed from selected data in the U.S. Department of Commerce, Regional Economic Measurement Division, "State Personal Income, 1929-81: Revised Estimates," Survey of Current Business, (Washington: U.S. Government Printing Office, August 1982), p. 57; U.S. Department of Commerce, Bureau of Economic Analysis, Commerce News, Report BEA #83-21, (Washington: U.S. Department of Commerce, May 1983), Table 1; The National Education Association, Estimates of School Statistics: 1973-74, (Washington: National Education Association, Estimates of School Statistics: 1982-83, (Washington: National Education Association, January 1983), p. 39.

certainly not realistic, but generally a reliable indicator of how much money is available.

The District of Columbia towers above all other jurisdictions in this figuring. The District of Columbia's personal income per pupil in average daily attendance for 1982 was $116,859, which is 250 percent higher than a decade earlier. District of Columbia enrollment in public elementary and secondary schools also dropped more than for any state in the decade.

Among the 50 states, Connecticut, at $92,833, ranked highest in total personal income per pupil in average daily attendance, followed by New York, $90,819; Florida, $89,695; Delaware, $89,638; and New Jersey, $89,405.

Public Elementary and Secondary School Revenue Receipts

Total revenue receipts for public elementary and secondary education in the United States in 1982-83 came to an estimated $116.3 billion—almost 122 percent higher than a decade earlier, and $600 million less than total school expenditures in 1982-83. An additional $4 billion in non-revenue receipts—the amount received by local education agencies from the sale of bonds and real property and equipment, plus loans and proceeds from insurance adjustments—brought total receipts to $120.3 billion in 1982-83.

Revenue receipts for public elementary and secondary education for 1982-83, in adjusted 1972 dollars, totaled $50.6 billion. Compared to actual revenues in 1972-73 of $52.4 billion, revenue receipts decreased in purchasing power in 1982-83 by 3.6 percent, compared to a 1.6 percent decline in school expenditures in real dollars over the same period.

States that had the greatest increases in school revenue receipts during the past decade also showed, for the most part, the greatest boosts in personal income and school expenditures. Oklahoma actually increased school expenditures above revenue receipts over the past decade, although its 1982-83 school revenue receipts of $1,722,358,000 exceeded estimated expenditures of $1,690,901,000. States which increased revenue receipts the most in the last decade were: Wyoming, 286.8 percent; Alaska, 285.7 percent; Texas, 231.1 percent; Utah, 220.3 percent; New

TABLE 37. Personal income per pupil in ADA in 1972 and 1982 with percentage change, ranked by state's 1982 position

States	1982	1972	Percentage Change
1. District of Columbia	$116,859	$33,336	250.5
2. Connecticut	92,833	27,023	243.5
3. New York	90,819	30,870	194.2
4. Florida	89,695	24,330	268.7
5. Delaware	89,638	23,979	273.8
6. New Jersey	89,405	27,349	226.9
7. Illinois	85,376	27,509	210.4
8. Alaska	83,987	22,118	279.7
9. California	82,325	23,692	247.5
10. Rhode Island	82,286	25,224	226.2
11. Maryland	81,830	24,224	237.8
12. Pennsylvania	79,478	24,506	224.3
13. Massachusetts	78,578	25,335	210.2
14. Hawaii	77,918	25,476	205.8
15. Kansas	75,458	22,973	228.5
16. Nevada	73,172	22,884	219.8
17. Washington	72,000	21,362	237.0
18. Colorado	70,698	20,599	243.2
50 States and D.C.	70,422	22,380	214.7
19. Missouri	69,680	22,141	214.7
20. Wisconsin	69,163	21,579	220.5
21. Oregon	68,603	22,149	209.7
22. New Hampshire	68,569	21,078	225.7
23. Ohio	68,044	21,838	211.6
24. Minnesota	67,732	19,790	242.3
25. Virginia	66,911	21,251	214.9
26. Nebraska	66,892	21,779	207.1
27. North Dakota	64,164	20,071	219.7
28. Iowa	63,740	20,794	206.5
29. Texas	63,468	18,790	237.8
30. Wyoming	63,088	19,068	230.9
31. Oklahoma	62,813	17,652	255.8
32. Louisiana	62,657	16,976	269.1
33. Michigan	62,104	21,450	189.5
34. Indiana	61,973	20,830	197.5
35. Montana	57,809	18,417	213.9
36. Vermont	57,151	18,662	206.2
37. Arizona	56,850	19,496	191.6
38. South Dakota	55,627	17,015	226.9
39. Georgia	55,008	19,091	188.1
40. Kentucky	53,985	18,232	196.1
41. Tennessee	53,117	18,004	195.0
42. North Carolina	53,070	18,747	183.1
43. Maine	52,235	16,133	223.8
44. West Virginia	49,980	16,887	196.0
45. Alabama	48,423	16,458	194.2
46. New Mexico	47,838	14,593	227.8
47. South Carolina	47,484	16,404	189.5
48. Arkansas	46,698	16,076	190.5
49. Idaho	46,455	17,093	171.8
50. Mississippi	45,327	14,421	214.3
51. Utah	39,754	14,701	170.4

SOURCE: Computed from selected data in the U.S. Department of Commerce, Regional Economic Measurement Division, State Personal Income, 1929-81: Revised Estimates," Survey of Current Business, (Washington: U.S. Government Printing Office, August 1982), p. 53; The National Education Association, Estimates of School Statistics: 1973-74 (Washington: National Education Association, 1974), p. 26; U.S. Department of Commerce, Bureau of Economic Analysis, Commerce News, Report BEA #83-21, (Washington: U.S. Department of Commerce, May 1983), Table 3; and The National Education Association, Estimates of School Statistics: 1982-83, (Washington: National Education Association, January 1983), p. 32.

TABLE 38. Total revenue receipts for public elementary and secondary schools and percentage change, by state: 1972-1973 and 1982-83

States	1972-73	1982-83	Percentage Change
50 States and D.C.	$52,427,126	$116,273,471	121.8
Alabama	500,230	1,144,813	123.9
Alaska	155,273	598,852	285.7
Arizona	476,420	1,400,000	193.9
Arkansas	308,084	930,232	201.9
California	6,162,289	9,545,394	54.9
Colorado	666,524	1,812,800	172.0
Connecticut	935,110	1,814,518	94.0
Delaware	186,909	361,489	93.4
District of Columbia	221,010	319,839	44.7
Florida	1,468,906	4,200,000	187.9
Georgia	829,275	2,440,751	194.3
Hawaii	237,335	510,676	115.2
Idaho	154,665	460,500	197.7
Illinois	3,169,690	6,117,657	93.0
Indiana	1,238,712	2,665,432	115.2
Iowa	714,275	1,508,199	111.2
Kansas	515,805	1,365,141	164.7
Kentucky	568,818	1,494,000	162.6
Louisiana	796,998	1,917,620	140.6
Maine	217,425	552,847	154.3
Maryland	1,345,994	2,380,831	76.9
Massachusetts	1,386,500	2,900,000	109.2
Michigan	2,430,000	5,725,030	135.6
Minnesota	1,250,000	2,416,500	93.3
Mississippi	400,381	991,172	147.6
Missouri	1,025,949	2,165,565	111.1
Montana	162,700	486,841	199.2
Nebraska	300,410	680,737	126.6
Nevada	134,500	358,499	166.5
New Hampshire	160,501	406,000	153.0
New Jersey	2,204,000	4,865,356	120.8
New Mexico	272,600	830,100	204.5
New York	6,040,000	10,709,000	77.3
North Carolina	1,071,761	2,640,583	146.4
North Dakota	136,400	340,500	149.6
Ohio	2,354,844	5,251,000	115.4
Oklahoma	516,719	1,722,358	123.0
Oregon	547,315	1,633,282	198.4
Pennsylvania	3,031,052	6,312,000	108.2
Rhode Island	213,206	471,461	121.1
South Carolina	533,673	1,376,662	158.0
South Dakota	147,657	344,000	133.0
Tennessee	704,678	1,868,282	165.1
Texas	2,483,529	8,222,605	231.1
Utah	266,351	853,136	220.3
Vermont	136,330	278,412	104.2
Virginia	1,093,983	2,682,505	145.2
Washington	955,318	2,237,380	134.2
West Virginia	334,482	970,446	190.1
Wisconsin	1,175,586	2,617,468	122.7
Wyoming	96,954	375,000	286.8

SOURCE: Selected data from The National Education Association, Estimates of School Statistics: 1973-74, (Washington: National Education Association, 1974), p. 32; and Estimates of School Statistics: 1982-83, (Washington: National Education Association, January 1983), p. 37.

Mexico, 204.5 percent; Arkansas, 201.9 percent; Arizona, 193.9 percent; Oregon, 198.4 percent; Oklahoma, 123.0 percent.

In real (1972) dollars, several states had a substantial decrease in revenue receipts for public elementary and secondary schools in the past ten years.

Sources of Revenue for Public Elementary and Secondary Schools

Financing public education in this country varies greatly from state to state and it changes constantly within the states. One of the most dramatic changes in the past decade has to do with the sources of revenue for public education—the shift away from local sources to the states. All but eight states recorded a decrease in local share of education costs and an increase in state share in the past decade (Table 39).

The trend is reflected in the national averages. In 1972-73, states contributed 40.6 percent of public elementary and secondary school revenue receipts. Local and "other" sources came up with 51.5 percent, and the federal government, 7.9 percent. In 1982-83, the proportion of total revenue receipts for public elementary and secondary education from states had increased to 50.3 percent. From local sources, it had decreased to 42.3 percent. The federal share dropped to 7.4 percent in 1982-83.

States showing the most dramatic shifts in source of public school revenue between 1972-73 and 1982-83 were California, Connecticut, Idaho, Indiana, Iowa, Kansas, Kentucky, Maine, Maryland, Massachusetts, Michigan, Minnesota, Montana, Nebraska, Nevada, New Jersey, New Mexico, North Dakota, Oklahoma, Oregon, South Dakota and Washington.

In California the local share of public school education revenue went from 58.6 percent in 1972-73 to 8.9 percent in 1982-83, and the state share rose from 34.0 percent to 85.8 percent, while the federal share decreased from 7.4 percent to 5.3 percent. Idaho's state share jumped from 39.4 percent to 62.6 percent for the decade, while the local share decreased from 48.5 percent to 30.4 percent and the federal share from 12.1 percent to 6.9 percent.

Oklahoma's state share increased from 42.9 percent to 60.2 the last decade; the local contribution fell from 47.3 percent to 29.5 percent; and the federal

TABLE 39. Percentage of elementary and secondary school revenue receipts by source, by state: 1972–73 and 1982–83

State	1972-73			1982-83		
	Federal	State	Local and Other	Federal	State	Local and Other
50 States and D.C.	7.9	40.6	51.5	7.4	50.3	42.3
Alabama	17.0	64.0	19.0	14.8	64.3	21.0
Alaska	15.2	67.8	17.0	5.7	78.3	16.0
Arizona	8.2	41.6	50.3	11.4	45.7	42.9
Arkansas	15.3	48.0	36.7	13.3	54.3	32.4
California	7.4	34.0	58.6	5.3	85.8	8.9
Colorado	7.0	26.9	66.1	5.4	36.9	57.7
Connecticut	3.1	23.1	73.8	4.9	36.4	58.7
Delaware	7.5	69.6	23.0	11.2	67.6	21.2
District of Columbia	12.9	----	87.1	15.5	----	84.5
Florida	9.8	55.3	34.9	7.1	61.9	31.0
Georgia	12.5	53.4	34.1	10.2	55.6	34.2
Hawaii	8.5	88.5	3.0	9.9	89.8	0.3
Idaho	12.1	39.4	48.5	6.9	62.6	30.4
Illinois	6.0	36.9	57.1	8.5	38.0	53.4
Indiana	5.1	31.5	63.5	6.3	58.6	35.1
Iowa	4.8	34.6	60.6	7.3	42.1	50.6
Kansas	8.0	27.4	64.6	4.8	44.4	50.8
Kentucky	14.9	55.3	29.8	10.7	70.5	18.7
Louisiana	13.7	56.0	30.2	9.4	55.9	34.7
Maine	9.3	34.5	56.2	10.1	49.7	40.2
Maryland	6.9	47.8	45.3	5.9	40.2	53.9
Massachusetts	5.2	24.2	70.7	4.8	39.4	55.8
Michigan	3.8	47.6	48.6	8.1	36.1	55.8
Minnesota	4.7	58.0	37.2	4.7	48.9	46.3
Mississippi	26.9	49.0	24.1	23.0	53.3	23.7
Missouri	8.0	35.1	56.9	8.1	39.6	52.3
Montana	8.5	25.2	66.3	8.5	47.4	44.2
Nebraska	8.5	15.6	75.9	7.1	27.9	65.0
Nevada	6.7	37.8	55.5	7.6	60.6	31.8
New Hampshire	4.8	7.6	87.5	3.9	6.9	89.2
New Jersey	5.8	26.2	68.1	3.5	40.0	56.4
New Mexico	20.5	60.0	19.6	10.2	77.8	12.0
New York	5.4	40.6	54.0	4.0	41.9	54.1
North Carolina	15.4	64.1	20.5	16.1	61.5	22.4
North Dakota	10.7	28.8	60.5	7.3	51.5	41.1
Ohio	5.8	33.3	60.9	5.0	40.7	54.3
Oklahoma	9.8	42.9	47.3	10.3	60.2	29.5
Oregon	4.3	20.3	75.5	8.8	36.8	54.4
Pennsylvania	7.8	50.6	41.6	7.5	45.2	47.4
Rhode Island	7.7	35.8	56.5	4.7	37.0	58.3
South Carolina	17.0	55.7	27.3	13.6	57.1	29.3
South Dakota	11.9	13.5	74.6	8.7	27.6	63.7
Tennessee	13.1	45.1	41.9	13.0	47.2	39.8
Texas	12.0	46.9	41.2	10.0	50.6	39.5
Utah	9.1	53.1	37.8	5.2	56.3	38.5
Vermont	6.1	33.0	60.9	7.0	35.2	57.8
Virginia	10.4	34.5	55.0	6.6	41.6	51.8
Washington	8.7	47.2	44.0	5.4	75.2	19.4
West Virginia	12.9	56.8	30.3	9.0	62.4	28.5
Wisconsin	3.9	30.6	65.5	5.4	37.4	57.2
Wyoming	9.3	33.8	56.9	4.0	34.7	61.3

SOURCE: Selected data from The National Education Association, _Estimates of School Statistics: 1973-74_, (Washington: National Education Association, 1974), p. 32; and _Estimates of School Statistics: 1982-83_, (Washington: National Education Association, January 1983), p. 37.

contribution stayed about the same—10.3 percent, compared with 9.8 percent in 1972-73.

Twenty-three states picked up more than half of the cost of public elementary and secondary education in their states last year, compared to 14 in 1972-73 (Table 40).

Five states actually contributed more than three-fourths of the costs of public elementary and secondary education in their states in 1982-83: Hawaii, 89.8 percent; California, 85.8 percent; Alaska, 78.3 percent; New Mexico, 77.8 percent; and Washington, 75.2 percent.

Federal Share of Public Elementary and Secondary Education

There is great variation in the federal share of public elementary and secondary school revenue from state to state—from a high of 23.0 percent in Mississippi to a low of 3.5 percent in New Jersey. Southern states got the greatest share of federal funds both in 1972-73 and in 1982-83 Southern states also rank among the lowest in per-pupil expenditures and per-capita income. However, significant gains have been made in the South in raising per-pupil expenditures in the past decade. Per-capita income in most Southern states also is on the rise.

Salaries of Teachers Compared With Salaries of other Employees

According to the National Education Association, the average starting salary of a public elementary or secondary school teacher with a bachelor's degree was $12,769 in 1981-82.[26] It was almost $3,500 less than the starting salary of the next lowest profssional—$16,200 for a college graduate in business administration. The highest beginning salary for a person with a bachelor's degree that year was $20,364—in computer sciences. A beginning teacher's salary also showed the smallest gain since 1973-74, except for accountants, having increased by only 65.4 percent, whereas the average beginning salary of every other professional, except beginning accountants, had gone up by more than 75 percent in the ten years (Table 41).

The gap between the salary of a teacher and that of other white-collar professionals widens considerably the longer a teacher is in the profession. A

TABLE 40. States ranked by sources of revenue receipts — federal, state, and local and other: 1982-83

Federal		State		Local and Other	
Mississippi	23.0	Hawaii	89.8	New Hampshire	89.2
North Carolina	16.1	California	85.8	District of Columbia	84.5
District of Columbia	15.5	Alaska	78.3	Nebraska	65.0
Alabama	14.8	New Mexico	77.8	South Dakota	63.7
South Carolina	13.6	Washington	75.2	Wyoming	61.3
Arkansas	13.3	Kentucky	70.5	Connecticut	58.7
Tennessee	13.0	Delaware	67.6	Rhode Island	58.3
Arizona	11.4	Alabama	64.3	Vermont	57.8
Delaware	11.2	Idaho	62.6	Colorado	57.7
Kentucky	10.7	West Virginia	62.4	Wisconsin	57.2
Oklahoma	10.3	Florida	61.9	New Jersey	56.4
Georgia	10.2	North Carolina	61.5	Massachusetts	55.8
New Mexico	10.2	Nevada	60.6	Michigan	55.8
Maine	10.1	Oklahoma	60.2	Oregon	54.4
Texas	10.0	Indiana	58.6	Ohio	54.3
Hawaii	9.9	South Carolina	57.1	New York	54.1
Louisiana	9.4	Utah	56.3	Maryland	53.9
West Virginia	9.0	Louisiana	55.9	Illinois	53.4
Oregon	8.8	Georgia	55.6	Missouri	52.3
South Dakota	8.7	Arkansas	54.3	Virginia	51.8
				Kansas	50.8
Illinois	8.5	Mississippi	53.3	Iowa	50.6
Montana	8.5	North Dakota	51.5	Pennsylvania	47.4
Michigan	8.1	Texas	50.6	Minnesota	46.3
Missouri	8.1	**50 States and D.C.**	50.3	Montana	44.2
Nevada	7.6	Maine	49.7	Arizona	42.9
Pennsylvania	7.5	Minnesota	48.9	**50 States and D.C.**	42.3
50 States and D.C.	7.4	Montana	47.4	North Dakota	41.1
Iowa	7.3	Tennessee	47.2	Maine	40.2
North Dakota	7.3	Arizona	45.7	Tennessee	39.8
Nebraska	7.1	Pennsylvania	45.2	Texas	39.5
Florida	7.1	Kansas	44.4	Utah	38.5
Vermont	7.0	Iowa	42.1	Indiana	35.1
Idaho	6.9	New York	41.9	Louisiana	34.7
Virginia	6.6	Virginia	41.6	Georgia	34.2
Indiana	6.3	Ohio	40.7	Arkansas	32.4
Maryland	5.9	Maryland	40.2	Nevada	31.8
Alaska	5.7	New Jersey	40.0	Florida	31.0
Colorado	5.4	Missouri	39.6	Idaho	30.4
Wisconsin	5.4	Massachusetts	39.4	Oklahoma	29.5
Washington	5.4	Illinois	38.0		
California	5.3	Wisconsin	37.4	South Carolina	29.3
Utah	5.2	Rhode Island	37.0	West Virginia	28.5
Ohio	5.0	Colorado	36.9	Mississippi	23.7
Connecticut	4.9	Oregon	36.8	North Carolina	22.4
Kansas	4.8	Connecticut	36.4	Delaware	21.2
Massachusetts	4.8	Michigan	36.1	Alabama	21.0
Minnesota	4.7	Vermont	35.2	Washington	19.4
Rhode Island	4.7	Wyoming	34.7	Kentucky	18.7
New York	4.0	Nebraska	27.9	Alaska	16.0
Wyoming	4.0	South Dakota	27.6	New Mexico	12.0
New Hampshire	3.9	New Hampshire	6.9	California	8.9
New Jersey	3.5	District of Columbia	NA	Hawaii	0.3

SOURCE: Selected data from The National Education Association, Estimates of School Statistics: 1982-83, (Washington: National Education Association, January 1983), p. 37.

TABLE 41. Average starting salaries of public school teachers compared with starting salaries in private industry: 1873-74, 1980-81, and 1981-82

Position/Field	1973-74	1980-81	1981-82	Percentage change 1981-82 over 1980-81	Percentage change 1981-82 over 1973-74
Average minimum mean salary for teachers with bachelor's degrees	$ 7,720	$11,758	$12,769	8.6	65.4
College graduates with bachelor's degrees					
Engineering	11,220	20,136	22,368	11.1	99.3
Accounting	10,632	15,720	16,980	8.0	59.7
Sales-Marketing	9,660	15,936	17,200	8.1	78.3
Business Administration	8,796	14,100	16,200	14.9	84.2
Liberal Arts	8,808	13,296	15,444	16.2	75.3
Chemistry	10,308	17,124	19,536	14.1	89.5
Math-Statistics	10,020	17,604	18,600	5.7	85.6
Economics-Finance	9,624	14,472	16,884	16.7	75.4
Computer Sciences	NA	17,712	20,364	15.0	NA
Other Fields	9,696	17,544	20,028	14.2	106.6

SOURCE: Selected data from The National Education Association, <u>Prices, Budgets, Salaries, and Income: 1981</u>, (Washington: National Education Association, 1981); and <u>Prices, Budgets, Salaries, and Income: 1983</u>, (Washington: National Education Association, 1983), p. 22.

TABLE 42. Average annual earnings of full-time city employees and average salaries of public school teachers, by state: 1974, 1980, and 1981

Function	1974	1980	1981	Percentage Change 1981 over 1980	Percentage Change 1981 over 1974
Average teacher's salary	$11,690	$16,511	$18,115	9.7	55.0
City Employees:					
All functions	11,232	16,368	18,348	12.1	63.4
Highways	9,528	13,980	15,612*	11.7	63.9
Public welfare	9,996	14,004	16,032*	14.5	60.4
Hospitals	9,132	13,116	14,976*	14.2	64.0
Health	10,248	15,960	18,408	15.3	79.6
Police protection	12,180	17,748	20,148	13.5	65.4
Fire protection	12,864	19,008	21,600	13.6	67.9
Sewerage	9,684	14,940	16,596*	11.1	71.4
Sanitation	9,324	13,644	15,048*	10.3	61.4
Parks & Recreation	9,204	13,452	14,472*	7.6**	57.2
Housing/Urban Renewal	12,756	15,576	17,772*	14.1	39.3**
Airports	10,380	16,188	17,736*	9.6**	70.9
Water Transport and Terminals	12,888	19,968	23,772	19.1	84.5
Correction	12,468	18,192	21,144	16.2	69.6
Libraries	8,712	13,152	14,460*	9.9	66.0
Financial Administration	9,852	14,712	16,212*	10.2	64.6
General Control	10,956	16,020	17,556*	9.6**	60.2
Local Utilities	11,628	17,592	19,608	11.5	68.6
Water Supply	9,864	15,048	17,016*	13.1	72.5
Electric Power	11,772	18,396	20,808	13.1	76.8
Transit	14,616	21,036	22,954	9.1**	57.0
Gas Supply	9,732	13,620	14,736*	8.2**	51.4**
All other functions	10,356	14,376	16,800*	16.9	62.2

*   Average salary less than that of teachers
** Percentage increase lower than that for teachers

SOURCE: Selected data from The National Education Association, <u>Prices, Budgets, Salaries, and Income: 1983</u>, (Washington: National Education Association, 1983), p. 19.

TABLE 43. Average salaries paid full-time employees of state and local governments compared with average salaries paid teachers, by state: 1971-72 and 1981-82

State	Government Employees			Teachers		
	1971	1981	Percent Increase	1971-72	1981-82	Percent Increase
Alabama	$ 6,744	$14,220	110.9	$ 7,737	$15,600	101.6
Alaska	13,236	28,728	117.0	14,124	31,924	126.0*
Arizona	9,072	19,104	110.6	9,915	18.014	81.7
Arkansas	5,964	12,936	116.9	6,843	14,506	112.0
California	10,908	22,428	105.6	11,417	22,755	99.3
Colorado	8,256	18,504	124.1	9,264	19,577	111.3
Connecticut	9,780	16,884	72.6	10,295	18,880	83.4*
Delaware	8,172	16,320	102.2	10,420	19,290	85.1
Florida	7,740	15,456	99.7	8,935	16,780	87.8
Georgia	6,684	13,884	107.7	7,926	16,363	106.4
Hawaii	9,432	18,372	94.8	10,320	22,542	118.4
Idaho	6,888	15,252	121.6	7,392	16,401	121.9*
Illinois	9,672	19,164	98.1	10,624	21,020	97.9
Indiana	7,908	15,612	97.4	9,755	18,622	90.9
Iowa	8,088	16,728	106.8	9,207	17,989	95.4
Kansas	7,260	14,988	106.4	8,251	16,712	102.5
Kentucky	7,152	15,108	111.2	7,362	17,290	134.9*
Louisiana	6,984	14,964	114.3	8,767	18,500	111.0
Maine	7,044	14,400	104.4	8,545	15,105	76.8
Maryland	9,192	18,504	101.3	10,463	21,210	101.9*
Massachusetts	9,264	17,280	86.5	10,176	18,787	84.6
Michigan	10,524	21,480	104.1	11,620	22,351	92.3
Minnesota	9,384	17,976	91.6	10,219	19,907	94.8*
Mississippi	5,724	12,420	117.0	6,530	14,135	116.5
Missouri	7,644	14,448	89.0	8,688	15,413	88.9
Montana	7,620	16,188	112.4	8,514	17,770	108.7
Nebraska	7,224	15,492	114.5	8,454	15,470	96.0
Nevada	8,952	18,696	108.8	10,200	20,105	97.1
New Hampshire	7,560	14,424	90.8	8,453	14,701	73.9
New Jersey	9,564	18,276	91.1	10,725	19,910	85.6
New Mexico	7,188	15,432	114.7	8,238	18,690	126.9*
New York	10,404	20,088	93.1	11,830	23,437	98.1*
North Carolina	7,968	14,784	85.5	8,593	16,947	97.2*
North Dakota	7,452	18,360	146.4	7,587	17,686	133.1
Ohio	8,412	16,548	97.1	8,772	18,550	111.5*
Oklahoma	6,828	14,292	109.3	7,647	16,210	112.0*
Oregon	8,844	18,540	109.6	9,485	20,305	114.1*
Pennsylvania	8,484	17,400	105.1	9,903	19,482	96.7
Rhode Island	8,448	18,720	121.6	9,910	21,659	118.6
South Carolina	6,528	14,304	119.1	7,355	15,170	106.3
South Dakota	6,888	14,124	105.1	7,678	14,717	91.7
Tennessee	6,780	14,664	116.3	7,990	16,285	103.8
Texas	7,164	15,984	123.1	8,472	17,582	107.5
Utah	7,896	16,476	108.7	8,460	18,152	114.6*
Vermont	8,040	14,844	84.6	8,462	14,715	73.9
Virginia	7,656	15,876	107.4	9,084	17,008	87.2
Washington	9,396	20,700	120.3	10,175	22,954	125.6*
West Virginia	6,888	14,472	110.1	8,103	17,129	111.4*
Wisconsin	9,204	18,360	99.5	10,016	19,387	93.6
Wyoming	7,368	18,300	148.4	9,234	21,249	130.1
United States	8,760	17,568	100.5	9,705	19,142	97.2

* Average salary of teachers increased more than that of government employees in these states.

SOURCE: Selected data from The National Education Association, _Prices, Budgets, Salaries, and Income: 1983_, (Washington: National Education Association, 1983), p. 18.

teacher starting out at $13,000 per year might be making $25,000 after fifteen years, whereas an accountant starting at $16,000 could easily be getting $50,000 to $60,000 after fifteen years.[27]

Even though classroom teachers would seem to make far less than accountants, computer scientists, engineers, and economists, they compare very well with federal, state, and city employees. The average teacher salary in 1981 was above that of 14 of 22 categories of city employees. The only municipal occupations that paid better than teaching were: health officials, policemen, firemen, water transport and terminal employees, and people working in the corrections, local utilities, electric power, and transportation fields.

Teachers in every state make more, on the average, than employees of a state or local government employee (Table 43). The average salary of a state or local government employee in 1981-82 was $17,568, compared to $19,142 for a classroom teacher. The average teacher salary also was higher than that of state and local government employees in 1971—$9,705 teachers compared to $8,760 for state and local government employees. However, the average increase in salaries for state and local government workers from 1971 to 1981 was slightly higher than for teachers—100.5 percent, compared to teachers' 97.2 percent increase over the decade.

CHAPTER V

Who is Going into the Profession

All the data about who currently is going into the teaching profession are grim. Not only are far fewer persons choosing teaching as a career, but the academic caliber of those who are is decreasing.

The reasons for the decline in quantity and quality of those electing to become classroom teachers are not hard to understand: low pay, poor working conditions, little opportunity for upward mobility within the profession, and lack of status in the society.

In addition, enrollments of students in elementary and secondary schools have been declining because of a drop in birth rates in the United States in the 1960s and most of the 1970s, reducing the demand for teachers. However, due to a baby boomlet in the late 1970s, an upturn in enrollments is forecast for pre-primary and elementary schools in the mid-1980s and for secondary schools in the late 1990s.[28] If current projections of people intending to go into teaching holds up, the country will experience a shortage of elementary teachers by the mid-1980s, just as the late 1970s bumper crop of babies is starting school.

Adding to this dilemma of teacher undersupply is the need for more qualified teachers to meet demands of a more rigorous curriculum called for by such reports as that of the National Commission on Excellence in Education.

At present, the outlook is not good for getting more and better qualified teachers to meet the new demands. Less than 5 percent of full-time college freshmen chose elementary or secondary school teaching as a probable career in 1982, compared to 19 percent in 1970.[29]

TABLE 44.   Total percent of first-time full-time freshmen
            indicating elementary or secondary school teaching as
            probable career occupation: Fall 1970 to 1982

Fall of Year	Elementary and Secondary School Teaching	Elementary School Teaching	Secondary School Teaching
1970	19.3	8.0	11.3
1971	15.4	6.8	8.6
1972	12.1	5.6	6.5
1973*	8.8	4.2	4.6
1974	7.7	3.5	4.2
1975	6.5	3.0	3.5
1976	8.0	4.3	3.7
1977	6.9	4.0	2.9
1978	6.2	3.7	2.5
1979	6.4	3.8	2.6
1980	6.0	3.8	2.2
1981	5.5	3.5	2.0
1982	4.7	3.0	1.7

* Specialist teaching included as a separate option in only the
  1973 survey. Inclusion of 3.9 percent responding that
  specialist teacher was probable career occupation would have
  increased total response to 12.7 percent.

SOURCE: The National Center for Education Statistics, The
          Condition of Education: 1983, (Washington: U.S.
          Government Printing Office, 1983), p. 218.

Data from the National Center for Education Statistics' National Longitudinal Study of 1972 and its High School and Beyond study in 1980 showed that 12 percent of the college-bound seniors said they intended to major in education in college in 1972 (Table 44). In 1980, only 7 percent chose education as an intended college major. Women comprised 75 percent of those signalling intent to major in education in both years. However, the number of female collegebound seniors declaring education as an intended college major dropped from 19 percent in 1972 to 10 percent in 1980.[30]

These data are substantiated by the fact that fewer than 5 percent of the high school seniors who took the Scholastic Aptitude Test (SAT) in 1982 said they intended to major in education at college--down 50 percent since 1973.[31]

Due to enrollment declines at elementary and secondary schools and contraction of class size to a manageable level, the demand for new teachers nationwide has been decreasing for about ten years.[32] The demand for secondary teachers will continue to decline throughout the 1980s because the population 14 to 17 years of age will continue to decline throughout this period, reducing secondary school enrollments. However, secondary school enrollments are expected to increase again in the mid-1990s, when the children of the baby boomlet of the late 1970s reach high school age.

Projections by the National Center for Education Statistics (NCES) indicate that the demand for additional teachers will exceed the supply of new teacher graduates in the years 1983 through 1987: by 8,000 in 1983, by 4,000 in 1984, by 28,000 in 1985, by 31,000 in 1986, and by 15,000 in 1987.[33]

Student enrollment is not the only variable affecting demand for teachers. In addition, efforts to keep student-teacher ratios down and replace teachers who leave the profession contribute to the demand. NCES projects increases in elementary school enrollments from 1986 to 1990 and foresees student-teacher ratios improving only slightly. Also, it expects a constant turnover rate of existing teachers (6 percent per year), with 197,000 additional teachers hired per year from 1986 to 1990. This represents an expected increase from 134,000 additional teacher hirings for each year from 1981 to 1985.[34]

Likewise, it is projected that the supply of graduating teachers will average a little over 200,000 per year during that period. However, if the percentage of new teacher graduates who enter the teaching profession resembles the number in 1980, then the annual supply of new teachers will average only about 160,000 per year, and thus a sizeable across-the-board shortage could evolve.[35]

Projections in terms of supply and demand are difficult, however, for a number of reasons. On the income side of the ledger, for example, there are many unemployed licensed teachers, a reserve pool from which school systems might draw. On the deficit side, many currently employed teachers indicate they would leave teaching now for any good opportunities elsewhere. Thus, it is difficult to project with a great deal of precision whether there will be a shortage in the teaching force in the immediate years ahead, and if so, to what extent.

There never has been, is not now, and probably never will be an across-the-board demand for teachers. But there has been, is, and will be a demand for teachers in certain regions of the country, in specific content areas and different grade levels.[36]

The demand for teachers throughout the 1980s and 1990s will shift as the number of students enrolled in American schools changes by grade level, region of the country, and ethnic background.

Demand for teachers in the 1980s will be heaviest in grades K-8. Secondary and undergraduate school enrollments are projected to decline throughout the 1980s and most of the 1990s.

College Enrollment Trends

Who is graduating now from institutions of higher education and going into the teaching profession is of critical importance. Overall, the number of college-age people in the country is expected to decline throughout this decade. However, the number of students enrolled in college is expected to continue to rise. The percentage of the population 18 to 24 years of age who enrolled in college increased from 26.1 percent in 1963 to 41.8 percent in 1981, with a slight percentage dip occurring during the recession of the late 1970s.

Recent surveys show that the number of persons 35 years of age and over enrolled in college rose by 36.8 percent between 1974 and 1979 (Table 45). College students between 25 and 34 years of age increased by 21.5 percent from 1974 to 1979.[37]

Also, more women, blacks and members of other minorities are going to institutions of higher education than ever before.

Degrees Conferred in Education

The total number of bachelor's degrees conferred in education has steadily decreased from 194,229 in 1973 to 108,309 in 1981. Education degrees represented 21.0 percent of all bachelor's degrees conferred in 1972. Education dropped to 11.6

TABLE 45. Total enrollment in institutions of higher education
compared with population aged 18-24, United States:
Fall 1963 to Fall 1981

Year	Population 18-24 years of age	Enrollment	Number enrolled per 100 persons 18-24 years of age
1	2	3	4
1963	18,268,000	4,765,867	26.1
1964	18,783,000	5,280,020	28.1
1965	20,293,000	5,920,864	29.2
1966	41,376,000	6,389,872	29.9
1967	22,327,000	6,911,748	31.0
1968	22,883,000	7,513,091	32.8
1969	23,723,000	8,004,660	33.7
1970	24,687,000	8,590,887	34.8
1970	24,687,000	8,580,887	34.8
1971	25,779,000	8,948,644	34.7
1972	25,913,000	9,214,860	35.6
1973	26,397,000	9,602,123	36.4
1974	26,916,000	10,223,729	38.0
1975	27,605,000	11,184,859	40.5
1976	28,163,000	11,012,137	39.1
1977	28,605,000	11,285,787	39.5
1978	28,971,000	11,260,092	38.9
1979	29,285,000	11,569,899	39.5
1980	29,462,000	12,096,895	41.1
1981	29,512,000	12,300,000	41.7

SOURCE: Selected data from The National Center for Education
Statistics, The Digest of Education: 1982,
(Washington: National Center for Education Statistics,
1982), p. 92.

TABLE 46. Earned degrees conferred in all discipline divisions and in education, by level and sex of recipient: 1970-71 and 1980-81

Year	Both Sexes Education Degrees			Male Education Degrees			Female Education Degrees		
	Total	Number	Percentage of Total	Total	Number	Percentage of Total	Total	Number	Percentage of Total
Bachelor's Degrees:									
1971	839,730	176,614	21.0	475,593	45,094	9.5	364,136	131,520	36.1
1981	935,140	108,309	11.6	469,883	27,076	5.8	465,257	81,233	17.5
Master's Degrees:									
1971	230,509	88,952	38.6	138,145	38,977	28.2	92,363	49,975	54.1
1981	295,739	98,938	33.3	147,043	28,256	19.2	148,696	70,682	47.5
Doctor's Degrees:									
1971	32,107	6,403	19.9	27,530	5,045	18.3	4,577	1,358	29.7
1981	32,958	7,900	24.0	22,711	4,164	18.3	10,247	3,736	36.5

SOURCE: Selected data from The National Center for Education Statistics, The Condition of Education: 1983,
(Washington: National Center for Education Statistics, 1982), p. 184.

percent of all bachelor's degrees awarded in 1980. Degrees in education went to 36.1 percent of all females awarded bachelor's degrees in 1971. In 1981, women receiving bachelor's degrees in education represented only 17.5 percent of all women awarded bachelor's degrees. Seventy-four percent of those receiving a bachelor's degree in education, however, were women.

From 1971 to 1976, the number of master's degrees conferred in education steadily increased (Table 46). Fewer persons chose education as a career in the last decade. Professionals already in education have gone on to get master's degrees, which are now a requirment in many states for teacher certification. Some teachers in K-12 classrooms are earning doctorates and leaving their current positions for opportunities in institutions of higher education or other professions where there is more money to be earned.

The percentage of master's degrees in education awarded to women increased from 57 percent in 1972 to 70 percent in 1980. Likewise, the percentage of doctorates in education awarded to women increased from 24 percent in 1972 to 44 percent in 1980. These data suggest the likelihood that women are staying in education as a profession longer than men, and many women are leaving elementary and secondary teaching to join the ranks of university professors and other higher-paying professions.

Of the 108,309 bachelor's degrees awarded in 1981 in education, 38,524 (35.6 percent) were in general elementary education, 2,973 (2.7 percent) in general secondary education, 4,807 (4.4 percent) in pre-elementary education, 13,950 (12.9 percent) in special education fields, and 19,095 (17.6 percent) in physical education.

The number of degrees conferred in several education fields changed dramatically from 1971 to 1981. For example: The number of bachelor's degrees conferred in elementary education dropped from 90,432 to 38,524, for a decrease of 57.4 percent. The number of degrees conferred in mathematics education dropped 64 percent—from 2,217 to 798. The number of degrees in science education decreased by one-third—from 891 to 597. Special education degrees rose from 8,360 to 13,950, for a 66.9 percent increase (Table 47).

TABLE 47. Earned bachelor's degrees conferred in education, by level and specialty: academic year 1970–71 and 1980–81

Specialty	1971	1981	Percentage Change
Education, total	176,614	108,309	−38.7
Education, general	2,026	2,777	37.1
Elementary education, general	90,432	38,524	−57.4
Secondary education, general	3,549	2,973	−16.2
Pre-elementary education	3,405	4,807	41.2
Junior high school education	721	248	−65.6
Higher education, general	6	5	−16.7
Junior and community college education	1	2	100.0
Adult and continuing education	12	25	108.3
Special education, all specialties	8,360	13,950	66.9
Special education, general	2,320	8,843	281.2
Administration of special education	0	20	−
Education of the mentally retarded	2,640	1,660	−37.1
Education of the gifted	12	28	133.3
Education of the deaf	239	349	46.0
Education of the culturally disadvantaged	3	22	633.3
Education of the visually handicapped	78	93	19.2
Speech correction	2,358	1,197	−49.2
Education of the emotionally disturbed	347	471	35.7
Remedial education	0	17	−
Special Learning disabilities	125	846	576.8
Education of the physically handicapped	149	137	−8.1
Education of the multiple handicapped	63	104	65.1
Education of exceptional children, not classified above	26	163	526.9
Social foundations	180	32	−82.2
Educational psychology	307	235	−23.5
Education statistics and research	3	0	−
Educational testing, evaluation, and measurement	0	50	−
Student personnel	7	299	417.4
Educational administration	5	27	440.0
Educational supervision	0	46	−
Curriculum and instruction	296	318	7.4
Reading education	9	370	401.1
Art education	5,661	2,392	−57.7
Music education	7,264	5,332	−26.6
Mathematics education	2,217	798	−64.0
Science education	891	597	−33.0
Physical education	24,732	19,095	−22.8
Driver and safety education	132	109	−17.4
Health education	1,089	2,259	107.4
Business, commerce, and distributive education	8,550	3,405	−60.2
Industrial arts, vocational and technical education	7,071	5,772	−18.4
Agricultural education	1,398	955	−31.7
Home economics education	6,449	1,767	−72.6
Nursing education	603	171	2.3
Teaching English as a foreign language	43	44	2.3
Other	1,195	925	−22.6

SOURCE: Selected data from The National Center for Education Statistics, The Condition of Education: 1983, (Washington: National Center for Education Statistics, 1982), p. 188.

TABLE 48. Percentage of women awarded degrees in
selected professions: 1950 to 1980

	1950	1955	1960	1965	1970	1975	1980
Doctors	10.4	4.7	5.5	6.5	8.4	13.1	23.4
Dentists	.7	.9	.8	.7	.9	3.1	13.3
Lawyers	NA	3.5	2.5	3.2	5.4	15.1	30.2
Engineers	.3	NA	.4	NA	.8	2.2	8.8
Education	46	64	64	67	67	68	71

SOURCE: Computed from selected data in U.S. Department of Commerce,
Bureau of the Census, Statistical Abstract of the United
States: 1981, 102 ed., (Washington: U.S. Government Printing
Office, 1981), p. 167.

Women in Education and Other Fields

Historically, women have carried the teaching force and continue to do so. Women
still constitute almost three-fourths of college majors in education. Females
represent 72 percent of those newly qualified to teach and 77 percent of new
teachers in 1980. However, more women generally are going to college, and the
best and brightest of them are getting degrees in fields other than teaching, as
women in record numbers choose professions that offer academic challenge, money,
and prestige. In 1980, 30.2 percent of law degrees were awarded to women,
compared to 3.2 percent in 1965, and 23.4 percent of new doctors were women,
compared to 6.5 percent 15 years earlier, while 8.8 percent of the engineering
degrees were awarded to women (Tables 48 and 49).

Women now constitute 52 percent of undergraduate enrollment. During
1960-1980, the percentage of college students who were males dropped from 65.5
percent to 49.7 percent, while the percentage of college enrollees who were women
increased from 34.5 percent to 50.6 percent.

In addition to concerns of status and prestige, sheer economic necessity is
driving women into higher paying professions. More than one in seven families (9.1
million) are headed by women, a 65 percent increase since 1970. A teaching salary
of $17,000 cannot support a household, many find.

TABLE 49. Degrees conferred in selected professions: 1960 to 1980
(First Professional Degrees for Medicine, Dentistry, Law)

Type of Degree	1960	1970	1980
Medicine (M.D.):			
Institutions conferring degrees	79	86	112
Degrees conferred, total	7,032	8,314	14,902
Men	6,645	7,615	11,416
Women	387	699	3,486
Dentistry (D.D.S. or D.M.D.):			
Institutions conferring degrees	45	48	58
Degrees conferred, total	3,247	3,718	5,258
Men	3,221	3,684	4,558
Women	26	34	700
Law (L.L.B. or J.D.):			
Institutions conferring degrees	134	145	179
Degrees conferred, total	9,240	14,916	35,647
Men	9,010	14,115	24,893
Women	230	801	10,754
Engineering:			
Degrees conferred, total	45,624	63,753	87,643
Men	45,453	63,227	80,001
Women	171	526	7,642
Bachelors[1]	37,679	44,479	68,893
Master's[2]	7,159	15,593	16,243
Doctorates	786	3,681	2,507
Education:			
Degrees conferred, total	124,523	250,696	229,495
Men	45,245	81,496	66,190
Women	79,278	169,200	163,305
Bachelor's	89,421	165,453	118,102
Master's	33,512	79,349	103,453
Doctorates	1,590	5,894	7,940

[1] Includes first professional

[2] Includes second professional or second level

SOURCE: Selected data from The National Center for Education Statistics, Digest of Education Statistics: 1982, (Washington: National Center for Education Statistics, 1982), pp. 118, 126, 127; and U.S. Department of Commerce, Bureau of the Census, Statistical Abstract of the United States: 1981, 101st ed., (Washington: U.S. Government Printing Office, 1981), p. 167.

TABLE 50. Elementary and secondary teaching status of recent bachelor's degree recipients newly qualified to teach, by field of teacher preparation: February 1978 and May 1981

Field of Teacher Preparation	Number Newly Qualified to Teach	Percentage Who Did Not Apply for Teaching Job	Total	Percentage of Those Who Applied for Teaching Job			
				Total Teaching	Teaching Full-Time	Teaching Part-Time	Not Teaching
1978:							
All fields	171,100	23	77	60	49	11	17
General elementary	46,100	13	86	71	58	13	16
Special education	23,300	14	85	72	64	9	13
Social science	12,300	25	75	55	45	10	20
Physical education	10,000	16	84	63	52	11	21
English	8,000	13	87	61	58	3	26
Music	7,200	23	77	57	38	19	20
Art	5,400	33	67	41	19	22	26
Mathematics	4,800	22	79	58	55	3	21
Vocational education	4,300	19	81	62	53	9	19
Business	3,700	52	49	39	34	4	10
Industrial arts	3,500	22	78	57	51	6	20
Other[a]	19,300	33	67	53	41	11	15
More than one field	22,200	40	60	39	30	9	20
No certification	1,000	NA	100	100	40	60	NA
1981:							
All fields	132,200	15	85	64	53	11	20
General elementary	36,400	11	89	71	60	11	18
Special eduation	16,500	12	88	75	70	4	13
Social science	7,400	17	83	63	54	9	20
Physical education	13,600	18	82	49	36	13	33
English	8,600	15	85	53	47	6	32
Music	8,200	19	81	59	50	9	21
Art	2,800	13	87	57	50	7	30
Mathematics	4,900	27	73	59	54	5	13
Vocational education	5,100	29	71	40	33	7	32
Business	3,300	24	76	38	31	7	38
Industrial arts	1,900	22	78	53	52	2	26
Biological science	2,500	11	89	83	68	15	6
Health	3,300	33	67	30	22	8	37
Home economics (nonoccupational)	2,100	10	90	64	54	10	25
Reading	1,600	6	94	65	62	3	29
Other[b]	5,400	23	77	53	41	12	25
More than one field	NA	NA	NA	NA	NA	NA	—
No certification	8,700	NA	100	100	54	46	0

[a] Data for the following fields are included in the "other" category because their sample numbers are too small to present them individually: biological science, foreign language, health, home economics (nonoccupational), reading, physical science, bilingual education, and English as a second language.

[b] Data from the following fields are included in the "other" category because their sample numbers are too small to present them individually: foreign language, physical science, bilingual education, English as a second language, and gifted and talented.

NOTE: Data exclude bachelor's recipients from U.S. Service Schools. Also do not include deceased graduates and graduates living at foreign addresses at the time of the survey.

SOURCE: The National Center for Education Statistics, The Condition of Education: 1983, (Washington: National Center for Education Statistics, 1982), p. 190.

TABLE 51. Recent bachelor's recipients newly qualified to teach in 1979-80 who were not teaching full-time in May 1981, by whether or not they applied to teach and current labor force status: May 1981

Status in May 1981	Number	Percentage Distribution, by Status	Percent Who Applied to Teach	Percent Who Taught in May 1980, but Not in May 1981	Percent Who Did Not Apply	Percent Not Reported
Total	[a]48,400	100.0	33.0	27.1	38.0	1.9
Employed:						
Professional, technical, managerial, and administrative workers excluding elementary/secondary teachers	18,400	38.0	32.3	20.9	44.1	2.7
Sales and clerical workers	7,300	15.1	35.6	18.4	43.6	2.4
All other workers	10,800	22.3	33.2	28.4	35.9	2.5
Unemployed	3,400	7.1	50.5	44.0	5.5	.0
In school	3,800	7.8	23.0	33.5	43.5	.0
Other, not in labor force	4,700	9.7	25.9	43.9	30.2	.0

[a] Excludes 4,000 for whom status is unknown

NOTE: Precision of the estimates may be calculated using the approximate coefficients of variation provided in the Data Sources in the Appendix

SOURCE: The National Center for Education Statistics, The Condition of Education: 1983, (Washington: National Center for Education Statistics, 1982), p. 214.

Those With Education Degrees Who Go On To Teach

Not all persons who get a degree in education become teachers. The annual supply of new teacher graduates decreased from 314,000 in 1971 to 132,000 in 1981. As a percentage of bachelor's degrees, new teacher graduates dropped from 37 percent to 12 percent over the same period.[38]

Between 1971 and 1981, bachelor's degrees in education decreased by 39 percent. The largest education field, general elementary education, declined by 57 percent.

And not all graduates qualified to teach apply for teaching positions. In 1979, of those newly qualified to teach, 23 percent did not apply for a teaching position. In 1981, this figure was 15 percent.[39] Ninety percent of those who did not apply said simply that they did not want to teach. Ten percent said teaching jobs were too hard to get, or they just didn't bother to apply. Of the 85 percent who did apply in 1981 for a teaching job, 20 percent wound up not teaching in the year following graduation (Table 50).

TABLE 52. Scholastic aptitude test (SAT) scores of college-bound seniors taking the SAT, by state: 1972 and 1982

States	1972		1982	
	SAT-Verbal	SAT-Math	SAT-Verbal	SAT-Math
United States	453	484	426	467
Alabama	419	441	463	501
Alaska	474	493	446	477
Arizona	507	533	470	511
Arkansas	486	511	480	519
California	464	493	425	474
Colorado	492	522	468	515
Connecticut	461	484	432	464
Delaware	458	485	432	465
District of Columbia	392	411	398	423
Florida	458	483	426	463
Georgia	405	429	394	429
Hawaii	433	488	392	465
Idaho	495	516	482	513
Illinois	475	507	462	515
Indiana	435	471	407	453
Iowa	526	565	516	572
Kansas	507	542	500	545
Kentucky	477	509	475	510
Louisiana	456	484	470	505
Maine	451	480	427	463
Maryland	454	482	425	464
Massachusetts	453	480	425	463
Michigan	458	493	459	514
Minnesota	509	547	485	543
Mississippi	413	438	479	509
Missouri	483	512	465	510
Montana	512	549	487	546
Nebraska	454	502	493	552
Nevada	485	511	436	481
New Hampshire	469	503	443	482
New Jersey	446	470	416	453
New Mexico	492	523	480	517
New York	460	495	429	467
North Carolina	411	438	396	431
North Dakota	525	566	505	563
Ohio	461	495	456	502
Oklahoma	495	522	483	518
Oregon	455	483	435	473
Pennsylvania	448	478	424	461
Rhode Island	451	476	420	457
South Carolina	399	424	378	412
South Dakota	513	546	522	553
Tennessee	479	508	480	519
Texas	445	476	415	453
Utah	525	554	494	528
Vermont	453	482	433	471
Virginia	444	475	426	462
Washington	492	521	468	514
West Virginia	469	499	462	506
Wisconsin	502	543	476	535
Wyoming	511	550	484	533

SOURCE: Selected data from state reports of the College Entrance Examination Board

Of those qualified but not teaching in the Spring of 1981, the largest proportion, 38 percent, were employed in managerial or other professional occupations (Table 51). Only 7.1 percent were unemployed.

Academic Caliber of Education Majors

Not only are fewer persons choosing teaching, but the caliber of those entering the teaching profession is low and continues to decline significantly. Data on intended education majors from the National Center for Education Statistics' National Longitudinal Study of 1972 and the High School and Beyond Study of 1980, showed that college aspirants who intended to major in education scored lower on standardized vocabulary, reading, and mathematic achievement tests than other college bound seniors. The prospective education majors also averaged lower high school grades and fewer courses in science and mathematics than students intending other majors.

Scholastic Aptitude Test scores in 1982 show that students embarking upon the study of education as a profession are less academically able than their collegiate colleagues. Future education majors had test scores well below those of entering students in the arts, the biological sciences, business, commerce and communications, physical sciences, and social sciences. The SAT scores of education majors were superior only to those of home economics, ethnic studies, and trade and vocational college-bound high school seniors. These low test scores effectively illustrate that the teaching profession, on the whole, is not attracting the better minds in American society.[40]

In 1973, high school seniors intending to major in education in college scored 27 points below the national average on the verbal portion of the SAT and 32 points below on the mathematics portion. By 1982, the gap between the average scores of college-bound education majors and the national averages had widened to 32 points on the verbal portion and 48 points on the mathematics portion of the SAT.

Average SAT scores across the nation declined steadily from 1973 with a slight upturn in 1982. However, SAT scores rose in the last decade in five states and the District of Columbia—and most of them in the South. Average SAT scores

TABLE 53. Profile of college-bound seniors who took the SAT, by state: 1982

State	Number Who Took the SAT	Number Who Took the SAT as Percentage of All Graduates	Percent from Non-Public Schools	Percent Minority	Percent Women	Percent Intended Education Majors
Alabama	2,990	6	30.4	20.2	51	2.9
Alaska	1,691	31	3.5	15.1	56	6.9
Arizona	3,352	11	19.1	11.8	50	2.8
Arkansas	1,221	4	13.6	9.4	48	2.9
California	102,261	36	17.0	32.5	53	4.1
Colorado	6,283	16	11.7	1.6	51	4.5
Connecticut	31,962	69	23.2	9.3	53	4.5
Delaware	4,602	42	32.1	13.8	52	4.7
District of Columbia	3,266	NA	47.4	67.6	50	2.6
Florida	37,879	39	19.5	15.3	52	4.4
Georgia	34,226	51	13.5	21.6	54	6.3
Hawaii	6,696	47	32.4	78.1	54	4.9
Idaho	908	7	7.9	5.5	50	4.5
Illinois	21,820	14	25.4	12.7	50	4.3
Indiana	37,331	48	9.8	9.5	53	7.1
Iowa	1,287	3	12.2	5.6	47	3.7
Kansas	1,602	5	16.1	8.2	48	4.2
Kentucky	2,920	6	28.0	7.4	47	3.1
Louisiana	2,743	5	53.6	20.0	50	3.4
Maine	7,898	46	14.3	2.8	52	8.0
Maryland	30,926	50	19.6	23.1	54	4.4
Massachusetts	56,435	65	19.3	8.0	50	3.9
Michigan	14,063	10	19.3	17.3	51	2.5
Minnesota	4,983	7	21.7	5.0	47	3.1
Mississippi	845	3	35.5	17.5	52	2.7
Missouri	7,185	10	32.3	13.3	49	4.1
Montana	1,007	8	6.3	3.0	48	3.1
Nebraska	1,388	5	16.4	6.9	51	4.0
Nevada	1,600	18	10.9	14.6	52	4.9
New Hampshire	7,795	56	21.9	4.2	51	5.6
New Jersey	69,741	64	19.4	16.2	51	5.3
New Mexico	1,497	8	20.5	22.1	54	3.0
New York	139,819	59	19.6	18.8	52	4.7
North Carolina	34,507	47	7.2	21.3	55	6.3
North Dakota	291	3	11.7	4.3	43	1.7
Ohio	25,042	16	28.5	9.3	49	4.6
Oklahoma	1,896	5	25.8	9.0	51	3.6
Oregon	12,708	40	7.9	8.3	53	7.5
Pennsylvania	87,039	50	21.4	9.3	52	5.5
Rhode Island	7,676	59	20.3	6.6	51	4.4
South Carolina	19,957	48	11.9	26.1	55	7.9
South Dakota	265	2	13.8	4.6	52	2.9
Tennessee	4,725	9	38.8	10.8	47	3.0
Texas	58,027	32	8.3	22.7	52	5.7
Utah	748	4	24.8	7.2	48	3.0
Vermont	4,028	54	15.8	2.8	53	7.8
Virginia	36,852	52	11.2	18.0	53	5.7
Washington	9,906	19	12.5	10.7	50	5.0
West Virginia	1,756	7	9.4	7.7	47	3.6
Wisconsin	7,432	10	22.7	6.3	48	3.6
Wyoming	339	5	3.0	3.9	55	5.0

SOURCE: Selected data from state reports of the College Entrance Examination Board

TABLE 54. Comparison of average SAT scores of college bound seniors in each state with those of college bound seniors intending to major in education: 1982

State	Average SAT Scores		Those Intending to Major in Education		Difference Between State Averages and Those Intending to Major in Education	
	Verbal	Math	Verbal	Math	Verbal	Math
United States	426	467	394	419	32	48
Alabama	463	501	400	428	63	73
Alaska	446	477	413	437	33	40
Arizona	470	511	440	449	30	62
Arkansas	480	519	420	445	60	74
California	425	474	399	424	26	50
Colorado	468	515	433	460	35	55
Connecticut	432	464	395	408	37	56
Delaware	432	465	389	409	43	56
District of Columbia	398	423	348	367	50	56
Florida	426	463	394	414	32	49
Georgia	394	429	366	393	28	36
Hawaii	392	465	365	418	27	47
Idaho	482	513	426	450	56	63
Illinois	462	515	423	455	39	60
Indiana	407	453	386	419	21	34
Iowa	516	572	473	478	43	94
Kansas	500	545	455	471	45	74
Kentucky	475	510	444	450	31	60
Louisiana	470	505	432	446	38	59
Maine	427	463	389	417	38	46
Maryland	425	464	394	415	31	49
Massachusetts	425	463	388	407	37	56
Michigan	459	514	423	451	36	63
Minnesota	485	543	443	475	42	68
Mississippi	479	509	404	406	75	103
Missouri	465	510	426	453	39	57
Montana	487	546	431	476	56	30
Nebraska	493	552	444	489	49	63
Nevada	436	481	398	420	38	61
New Hampshire	443	482	408	424	35	58
New Jersey	416	453	384	405	32	48
New Mexico	480	517	439	445	41	72
New York	429	467	405	433	24	34
North Carolina	396	431	365	393	31	38
North Dakota	505	563	NA	NA	NA	NA
Ohio	456	502	423	454	33	48
Oklahoma	483	518	442	448	41	70
Oregon	435	473	401	420	34	53
Pennsylvania	424	461	398	422	26	39
Rhode Island	420	457	393	415	27	42
South Carolina	378	412	356	384	22	28
South Dakota	522	553	490	531	32	22
Tennessee	480	519	446	475	34	44
Texas	415	453	385	406	30	47
Utah	494	528	430	463	64	65
Vermont	433	471	399	430	34	41
Virginia	426	462	388	408	38	54
Washington	468	514	431	454	37	60
West Virginia	462	506	397	411	65	95
Wisconsin	476	535	430	471	46	64
Wyoming	484	533	402	453	82	80

SOURCE: Selected data from state reports of the College Entrance Examination Board.

rose over the last ten years in Alabama, Louisiana, Michigan, Mississippi, Nebraska, Tennessee, and the District of Columbia (Table 52).

There is some reluctance to overplay SAT results—and with good reason. In some states, a very small proportion of high school seniors take the SAT, and usually it is the very brightest who do. Generally, the greater the percentage of a state's seniors who take the SAT, the lower that state's scores (Table 53).

However, there is one important conclusion to be drawn from an analysis of SAT scores of intended education majors in each state and that state's average SAT scores: without exception in all 50 states, regardless of what percentage of the state's high school graduates took the SAT, the scores of those intending to major in education fall considerably below a state's average SAT scores (Table 54).

The widest gap was in Mississippi, followed by West Virginia and then Iowa. The combined verbal and mathematics average of those intending to major in education in Mississippi was 810 in 1982. That is 178 points below Mississippi's average of 988. The combined SAT score of high school seniors intending to major in education in West Virginia fell 160 points below West Virginia's state average of 968. Iowa's intended education majors scored 137 points below the state's average of 1088, the highest combined 1982 SAT score in the nation.

South Carolina had the smallest gap between the average SAT score of its seniors intending to major in education and the average SAT score of all of its seniors who took the test in 1982. But South Carolina's combined verbal and mathematics average SAT score was 790, which was 103 points below the national average of 893. The average score of its intended education majors was 50 points lower, 740, the lowest combined SAT score in the nation for high school seniors intending to major in education.

CHAPTER VI

Teacher Education and Certification

Professional standards that apply to teacher education programs and the rules and regulations that govern certification decisions determine in large part the quality of beginning teachers in the United States. The quality of this teaching force clearly has been declining.

Teacher Testing

A recent movement to develop and use tests as some part of the certification and/or teacher education process will have a major impact on the quality of America's teaching force. In 1970, 21 states reported some use of proficiency examinations in the certification process. Several states reported use of the Modern Language Association (MLA) Examination for language teachers and/or as a substitute for required courses. The National Teacher Examination (NTE) used in some states was criticized in several cities, and at least one state has declared a moratorium on its use.[41]

In 1983, however, states are moving to institute tests at such a rapid rate that it is almost impossible to report the data before another state has decided to require a test as part of the certification requirements. These tests are taking several forms. Eight states are now testing the prospective teacher's basic skills as a prerequisite for entering the teacher education program--Alabama, Arizona, California, Colorado, Kansas, Missouri, New Mexico, and South Carolina. These states are either developing their own basic skills tests or are using the Educational

State	Certification Test Required	Type	Some Type of Test Under Consideration	
			Yes	No
Alabama	X	Basic Skills, certification		
Alaska				X
Arizona	X	Basic Skills	X	
Arkansas	X	NTE		
California	X	Basic Skills, Professional Knowledge		
Colorado	X	Basic Skills		
Connecticut			X	
Delaware	X	NTE		
Florida	X	Certification, Performance		
Georgia	X	Content, Performance		
Hawaii				X
Idaho				X
Illinois				X
Indiana				X
Iowa				X
Kansas	X	Basic Skills		
Kentucky			X	
Louisiana	X	NTE		
Maine				X
Maryland			X	
Massachusetts				X
Michigan				X
Minnesota				X
Mississippi	X	NTE		
Missouri	X	Basic Skills		
Montana				X
Nebraska				X
Nevada			X	
New Hampshire				X
New Jersey				X
New Mexico	X	Basic Skills		
New York			X	
North Carolina	X	NTE or GRE		
North Dakota				X
Ohio				X
Oklahoma	X	Certification, Performance		
Oregon			X	
Pennsylvania				X
Rhode Island				X
South Carolina	X	Basic Skills, Content, Performance		
South Dakota				X
Tennessee	X	NTE		
Texas			X	
Utah			X	
Vermont				X
Virginia	X	NTE	X	
Washington				X
West Virginia			X	
Wisconsin				X
Wyoming				X
Totals	18		11	23

SOURCE: Compiled by Feistritzer Publications, Washington, D.C.

Testing Service (ETS) PreProfessional Skills Test of Reading, Writing and Mathematics (Table 55).

Many states are now also requiring teachers to achieve a passing score on a content area test. Georgia, for example, requires teachers to pass a criterion-referenced test in their teaching fields, e.g., English, biology, elementary education.

Pedagogical examinations are also being required in some states. Florida had developed its own examination which includes a section on pedagogy. Also, the National Teachers Examination has been revised and a new Core Battery went into effect in 1982. That test consists of: 1) the Test of Communication Skills—reading, writing (including a sample), and listening; 2) the Test of General Knowledge—literature and fine arts, mathematics, science, and social studies; and 3) the Test of Professional Knowledge. It is very possible that as the Core Battery becomes better known it will be widely adopted. Validation studies are now underway in several states.

Some states are now assessing the performance of beginning teachers as part of the certification or contract renewal process. Three states—Georgia, Oklahoma, and Florida—are presently using performance tests for certification purposes. Two other states, South Carolina and Arizona, field tested performance instruments during 1982-83. In addition, Virginia, Connecticut, and Kentucky are actively moving towards the development and use of performance tests. Presently 18 states are using tests for certification purposes, and 11 are considering their own. Only 23 states indicated no interest. The total is more than 50 because some states that are already using tests are also considering the development and use of another test.

The development and use of tests is already having a impact upon the qualifications of those persons wishing to become teachers, particularly upon minority populations. Several years ago, Florida established a minimum score on the Scholastic Aptitude Test (SAT) and/or the American College Test (ACT) for the admittance of students to a teacher education program. The scores 835 and 17 respectively represent a minimum score at the 40th percentile. This has resulted in an overall reduction of 25 percent in the number of students entering teacher education programs and a reduction of approximately 90 percent in the number of minority candidates. The mean SAT score for students indicating that they wish to become teachers in 1982 was 813 twenty-two points below the minimum score to be admitted to a Florida teacher education program.

Florida has instituted another program that should have an impact upon the quality of the teaching force. According to legislation, any college or university must have at least 80 percent of its teacher education students pass the Florida Certification Examination or it will lose its approved program status. The results from the first year of this testing program have now been analyzed. Fifteen percent of the approved programs in Florida will be discontinued in 1983-84 because of the test scores of prospective teachers.

When Georgia instituted its content examinations, the highest passing rate (92 percent) was achieved by students who had majored in early childhood education programs. Since the test only included items that a teacher would be expected to know and teach to students up to the third grade, the data could be interpreted to mean that 8 percent of the graduating seniors in early childhood education programs were unable to pass an examination that covered content no more demanding than the content expected of a third grader.

These examples support the proposition that many of the lowest achieving students will be eliminated from competing for teaching positions. The testing movement now underway appears to have the potential for improving the quality of America's teaching force if only by raising the standard for the lowest acceptable candidates.

But these testing programs are not without problems. The most important impact clearly will be on minority populations. Already several projects are underway to improve the scores of minority candidates.

Liberal Arts Graduates

Another developing state policy may have an immediate impact on the teaching population. Several states have instituted policies allowing liberal arts graduates to begin teaching careers without any teacher preparation courses. While these people will be required to meet the state standards following their employment, they will be completing their first year of teaching without any formal preparation for these responsibilities. Advocates of this policy assume that certification policies have prevented qualified candidates from entering teaching careers. They also believe that teaching shortages in some areas such as math and science will be reduced if certification requirements are eliminated. It is too early to determine whether these policies will have the intended impact, but they do raise several related issues. If persons who have had no preparation as teachers are successful, will policy makers conclude that formal preparation programs are not needed, leading to the reduction or elimination of formal teacher education programs and possibly even state certification offices?

Output Standards

Tied to the development of teacher tests is a shift to "output standards for teacher education programs." During its last two national meetings, the National Association of State Directors of Teacher Education and Certification has discussed the development and use of output standards. Such an approach would place a greater emphasis on examining the graduates of the teacher education programs and less emphasis on examining the context and content of the program. In Florida and in Michigan new standards are being considered which place a greater emphasis on output measures.

The Florida program now being discussed would operate as follows: "The standard for approval of a teacher education program in Florida would be the successful completion of Florida's Beginning Teacher Program by 100 percent of the program's graduates." The Florida Beginning Teacher Program requires each school district to assist and assess the performance of the beginning teacher in relation to the 24 required Florida competencies.

An approved program will be discontinued when it is "determined through the review process that the performance of graduates is directly related to significant inadequacies in the teacher education program."[42]

The development of output standards will be based largely upon test data now being collected on graduates of approved programs. The development and use of tests as an essential part of the process used to certify teachers is clearly the

State	National Council of Accreditation of Teacher Education	National Association of State Directors of Teacher Education and Certification	Regional Accrediting Association	Specialty Organizations[a]	State Guides/ Standards	State Law
Alabama	X		X		X	
Alaska			X			
Arizona	X		X		X	
Arkansas						
California			X		X	
Colorado					X	
Connecticut	X	X	X			
Delaware		X				
Florida				X		
Georgia			X		X	
Hawaii		X	X		X	
Idaho		X				
Illinois					X	
Indiana	X		X		X	
Iowa					X	X
Kansas					X	
Kentucky	X	X			X	
Louisiana	X		X		X	
Maine					X	
Maryland	X	X				
Massachusetts					X	
Michigan		X			X	
Minnesota	X	X	X	X	X	
Mississippi	X					
Missouri	X		X		X	
Montana	X	X	X		X	
Nebraska	X				X __b	
Nevada						
New Hampshire						
New Jersey		X			X	
New Mexico	X		X		X	
New York					X	
North Carolina					X	
North Dakota	X		X		X	
Ohio			X	X	X	
Oklahoma					X	
Oregon	X	X	X			
Pennsylvania	X		X		X	
Rhode Island						
South Carolina						
South Dakota	X				X	
Tennessee	X	X	X	X	X	
Texas					X	
Utah	X	X			X	
Vermont	X				X	
Virginia	X	X	X	X		
Washington	X				X	
West Virginia						
Wisconsin		X		X	X	X
Wyoming	X		X			
Totals	24	17	20	6	34	2

a Subject matter and special program organizations, for example, the National Council of Teachers of Mathematics and the Council for Exceptional Children.

b Working on state approval process

SOURCE: Compiled by Feistrizer Publications, Washington, D.C.

most important development in the past thirteen years in the procedures used to certify teachers.

Teacher Certification

Professional school personnel in public elementary and secondary schools in every state are required by law or regulation to hold certificates issued by the designated legal authority (usually the state department or board of education) (Table 56). Three states—Minnesota, California, and Oregon—have separate state level commissions for teacher standards.[43] States exercise their authority over the certification of teachers by either approving collegiate programs of preparation or by reviewing the credentials of individual candidates to see that specific certification regulations are met. Forty-nine states do both. Only Mississippi does not approve programs.[44]

Since the majority of teachers in the United States have graduated from approved programs, the standards used to approve teacher education programs are of more significance than the individual certification requirements. States use one or more of the following standards to evaluate teacher education programs:

- o   National Council for Accreditation of Teacher Education
- o   National Association of State Directors of Teacher Education and Certification
- o   Regional Accrediting Association
- o   Specialty Organizations
- o   State Guides/Standards
- o   State Law

National Council for Accreditation of Teacher Education: The National Council for Accreditation of Teacher Education (NCATE) has been accrediting programs in teacher education for approximately 30 years. Originally established by a coalition representing the American Association of Colleges for Teacher Education (AACTE), the National Education Association (NEA), and the chief state school officers, NCATE was designed to protect the integrity of teacher education through peer assessment and self-regulation. While a minority of institutions (40 percent) belong to NCATE, a majority of the larger institutions are members. They represent about 80 percent of the candidates who become teachers. In the past few years NCATE has been reorganized and has taken a more vigorous role in declaring itself to be the "standard bearer" for the profession.

NCATE has established two levels of standards: basic for entry level programs and advanced for graduate or postbaccalaureate programs. The standards are organized into six broad categories. "Institutions are to determine objectives, decide who the students will be or describe who they are, collect appropriate faculty and physical resources to support the program, and evaluate the results in a systematic fashion. In addition, the entire enterprise must be under the control of a 'designated' unit of the faculty."[45] The major difference between NCATE and the state approval standards is that NCATE is voluntary while the state standards are mandatory.

National Association of State Directors of Teacher Education and Certification: The National Association of State Directors of Teacher Education and Certification (NASDTEC) Standards have been developed over the past 21 years. Beginning with the United States Office of Education Circular No. 351, Proposed Minimum Standards for State Approval of Teacher Preparing Institutions, the standards have been revised approximately every two years. Because the standards have been developed by state education personnel with responsibilities for teacher education and certification, the NASDTEC standards have been widely used in state approved program procedures. Twenty-six states have reported they use the NASDTEC standards in whole or in part. The standards address the organization and administration of teacher education, curriculum principles and standards for basic and advanced programs, innovative and experimental programs, and standards for approving competency-based or performance-based programs.

State Standards: State standards vary widely. In most cases, the state standards reflect the specificity in the individual certification regulations as well as features of the NCATE and NASDTEC standards. Examples of state standards follow:[46]

California: The Institution of Higher Education (IHE) must assure that programs address 27 competencies specified by the Commission. The IHE must also assure commitment of the chief administrator of the institution and involvement of practitioners in the certification area and members of the public in program development. IHEs must conduct graduate follow-up studies to be used in program revision, specify procedures to be used for evaluating candidates prior to certification, and conduct needs analyses in nearby school districts at least every four years.

Illinois: The state board has an elaborate set of program approval standards which, while granting maximum policymaking authority to IHEs, assure that the institutions have policies on a variety of issues often not mentioned in program approval in other states. For example, the IHE must document the need for the program, analyzing the available supply of teachers in the subject matter field and grade level, and demonstrate that the program is planned to develop capacities identified as important needs assessments of Illinois' public schools.

Interstate Certification: Eight states report that 65 percent of their beginning teachers came through approved programs within the states; 31 percent of their

TABLE 57.   Beginning teachers from selected state's own approved programs and from out of state: 1982

State	Number of beginning teachers	Number of beginning teachers from state's approved programs	Number of beginning teachers from out of state
Hawaii	505	497	8
Maryland	810	667	143
Michigan	950[a]	859	91
Montana	400	240	160
North Dakota	300	50	250
Utah	1445	873	178
Virginia	2962[a]	1402	1558

[a]1981-82 figures
[b]Estimates

SOURCE: National Education Association. Standards and Certification Bodies in the Teaching Profession (Washington, D.C.: 1983) p. 33

beginning teachers came from out of state. If this sample is representative of the rest of the country, approximately two-thirds of the country's beginning teachers come from in-state approved programs, with the majority of the remaining teachers coming from out of state, many of whom completed approved programs in other states (Table 57). These statistics vary widely from state to state. Almost all beginning teachers in Hawaii come from approved programs within the state while only one-sixth of the beginning teachers in North Dakota come through North Dakota's state approved programs.

The ease with which teachers can move from state to state has been facilitated by the Interstate Certification Project which is now administered by NASDTEC. Under the ICP agreements, a state enters into contractual agreements with other states. A recent survey revealed that 30 states now have some form of reciprocity with other states.[47]

Certification Requirements

Individual certification requirements vary from state to state (Tables 58 and 59). All states now require a bachelor's degree in order to get a license to teach. As recently as 1970 that was not the case. Only one state, Connecticut, requires more than a bachelor's degree in order to get a beginning teaching certificate at both the elementary and secondary levels. Seven states reported requiring at least a 2.5 grade point average in general education, the field of teaching specialty, and in pedagogy in order to be certified to teach. They are Connecticut, Hawaii, Kansas, Kentucky, Montana, New Jersey, and North Dakota.

Student Teaching

Thirteen states report requiring at least one semester of student teaching for elementary and secondary prospective teachers (Tables 60 and 61). Most student teachers have only one placement, with only three states reporting two placements for both elementary and secondary student teachers. States vary considerably in the length of time required for the student teaching experience--from five weeks in Missouri to fifteen weeks in Delaware. A student generally has one placement in his or her specialty and very little exposure to students from varied socioeconomic levels or bilingual or multicultural populations.

Certification Process

The policies that govern the certification process from state to state vary as much as the certification requirements (Table 62).

Forty-one states base their determination of who is certified to teach on whether or not the prospective teacher has a degree from a teacher preparation program previously approved by the state. Only four of the 45 states reporting—Hawaii, Missouri, Nevada, and Oklahoma—do not use the approved program approach in granting beginning teacher certificates.

Alabama and Oklahoma require passage of a state examination and North Carolina requires passage of the National Teacher Examination (NTE) of their in-state graduates. California, Nebraska, and Wyoming require passage of a state examination and Louisiana and North Carolina require passage of the NTE of their out-of-state prospective teachers.

Seventeen states issue a permanent teaching certificate to beginning teachers. They are California, Colorado, Connecticut, Delaware, Indiana, Massachusetts, Michigan, Missouri, Montana, New York, Ohio, Oklahoma, Pennsylvania, Texas, Utah, Washington, and Wisconsin.

Most states renew teaching certificates after five years. However, Louisiana and Pennsylvania renew the certificates of their teacher, after three years. Five states—Delaware, Iowa, Kentucky, Maryland, and Tennessee—report waiting ten years before a teacher comes up for certification renewal.

Twenty-one states require graduate credits before they will renew a teacher's certificate. Ten of these states also require in-service education hours. Four—California, Idaho, Illinois, and Ohio—require only that a fee be paid in order to renew a license to teach.

Certification in Field of Teaching

Nearly 94 percent of newly graduated full-time elementary and secondary school

TABLE 58. Requirements for initial teaching certificate: elementary, by State: 1983

State	Bachelor's	Bachelor's + 30	Bachelor's + Master's	General Education Percent of B.A.	General Education Minimum Achievement	Teaching Speciality Percent of B.A.	Teaching Speciality Minimum Achievement	Pedagogy Percent of B.A.	Pedagogy Minimum Achievement
Alabama	X			45	1.2	25	1.2	30	1.2
Alaska	X			—a		—a		—a	
Arizona	X			40	2.5	25	—a	20	—a
Arkansas *									
California	X			—a	—a	—a	—a	—a	—a
Colorado	X			40	2.0	60	2.0		
Connecticut	X	X	X	25	2.5	60	—a	25	2.5
Delaware *									
Florida	X			50	—a	10		40	
Georgia	X			(60 qh)	C	(45 qh)	C	(30 qh)	C
Hawaii	X			44	2.5	24	2.5	33	2.5
Idaho	X			20	2.0	30	2.0	30	2.0
Illinois	X			65	C	13	C	13	C
Indiana	X			—b	C	—b	C	24	C
Iowa *									
Kansas	X			35	2.5	10–15	2.5	10–15	2.5
Kentucky	X			33	2.5	25	2.5	25	2.5
Louisiana *									
Maine	X			25		—a	—a	—a	—a
Maryland	X			63		21		16	
Massachusetts	X			—a		—a			
Michigan	X								
Minnesota	X			—a		—a			
Mississippi	X			35		50		15	
Missouri	X								
Montana	X			50	2.5	25	2.5	20	2.5
Nebraska	X			25–50b	—a	50	—a	25	C
Nevada	X					—a			
New Hampshire *									
New Jersey	X			50	2.5	25	2.5	20	2.5
New Mexico	X			57	2.0	28	2.0–2.7	28	C–Ba
New York	X			—a		—a			
North Carolina	X			20	—a	40–60		20	
North Dakota	X			30	2.5	48	2.5	17	2.5
Ohio	X			—a		—a			
Oklahoma	X			42		20		17.5	
Oregon	X			—a		—a		—a	
Pennsylvania	X			—a		—a		—a	
Rhode Island *									
South Carolina *									
South Dakota	X			40	2.2	60	2.2		
Tennessee	X			(60 qh)		(36 qh)		(36 qh)	
Texas	X			30	—a	28	—a	24	—a
Utah	X			35–40	C+	30	C+	20	C+
Vermont	X								
Virginia	X			38		48		14	
Washington	X			—a		25		25	—a
West Virginia *									
Wisconsin	X			33	—a	(34/18sh)c		(26 sh)	—a
Wyoming	X			46		—a	C	20	C

qh = quarter hours
sh = semester hours
a Varies
b General Education and subject matter listed together
c Minimum of 34 semester credits for major, 18 for minor
* States did not respond to survey

SOURCE: National Education Association, Standard's and Certification Bodies in the Teaching Profession (Washington: 1983) p. 36

TABLE 59. Requirements for initial teaching certificate—Secondary, by state: 1983

	Degree			General Education		Teaching Speciality		Pedagogy	
State	Bachelor's	Bachelor's + 30	Bachelor's + Master's	Percent of B.A.	Minimum Achievement	Percent of B.A.	Minimum Achievement	Percent of B.A.	Minimum Achievement
Alabama	X			45	1.2	25	1.2	30	1.2
Alaska	X			--a		--a		--a	
Arizona	X			40	2.5	25	—a	20	--a
Arkansas*									
California	X			--a	--a	—a	—a	—a	--a
Colorado	X		X	40	2.0	60	2.0		
Connecticut	X	X	X	30	2.5	--a	—a	17	--a
Delaware	X								
Florida	X			50	--a	25	—a	25	--a
Georgia	X			(60 qh)	C	(45–50 qh)	C	(30 qh)	C
Hawaii	X			44	2.5	24	2.5	33	2.5
Idaho	X			20	2.0	30	2.0	30	2.0
Illinois	X			35	C	16	C	13	C
Indiana	X			32	C	29–34	C	19	C
Iowa	X								
Kansas	X			35	2.5	15–20	2.5	5–10	2.5
Kentucky	X			33	2.5	25	2.5	20	2.5
Louisiana*									
Maine	X			25		--a	—a	--a	--a
Maryland	X			55		30		15	
Massachusetts	X			--a	--a	—a	—a	--a	--a
Michigan	X								
Minnesota	X			--a	--a	—a	—a	--a	--a
Mississippi	X			35		50		15	
Missouri	X								
Montana	X			45	2.5	25	2.5–3.0	25	2.5–3.0
Nebraska	X			25–30b	--a	54	—a	16	--a
Nevada	X				--a				
New Hampshire*									
New Jersey	X			50	2.5	25	2.5	20	2.5
New Mexico	X			57	2.0	28	2.0–2.7	28	—a
New York	X			--a		--a	—a	--a	--a
North Carolina	X			20	--a	40–60		20	
North Dakota	X			30	2.5	48	2.5	17	2.5
Ohio	X			--a		--a			--a
Oklahoma	X			42		20–30		17.5	
Oregon*									
Pennsylvania	X			--a		--a		--a	
Rhode Island*									
South Carolina*									
South Dakota	X			40	2.2	60	2.2		
Tennessee	X			(60 qh)		(36 qh)		(36 qh)	
Texas	X			30	--a	38	—a	14	--a
Utah	X			35–40	C+	37	C+	17	C+
Vermont	X								
Virginia	X			43–53		27–41		16–20	
Washington	X			--a		15	—a	15	--a
West Virginia*									
Wisconsin	X			33	--a	(34/18sh)c		(18 sh)	--a
Wyoming	X			46					

qh = quarter hours
sh = semester hours
a Varies
b General Education and subject matter listed together
c Minimum of 34 semester credits for major, 18 for minor
* States did not respond to survey

SOURCE: National Education Association, Standards and Certification Bodies, 37

TABLE 60. Practicum: student teaching--elementary, by state: 1983

State	Length					Type of Student Teaching					
	One Semester	Number of Weeks	Number of Quarters	Number of Hours	Varies	Number of Placements	Teaching only in Specialty	Cross-Level Teaching	Across Socio-economic Levels	Bilingual/Multicultural	Varies
Alabama	X	10				1	X				
Alaska					X						X
Arizona					X						X
Arkansas											
California	X								X	X	
Colorado	X					1-2	X				
Connecticut				6-12sh							X
Delaware		15				1					
Florida		8-12				1		X	X		
Georgia	X					1	X				
Hawaii	X					1		X			
Idaho		8-12				2	X				
Illinois		6-9				1	X				
Indiana	X					1	X				
Iowa					X	1	X				
Kansas		8					X				
Kentucky		8									
Louisiana						1	X				
Maine					X						
Maryland		8-12				1					
Massachusetts				300 ch		1-2	X				
Michigan		10				1					
Minnesota					X						X
Mississippi		6				1	X				
Missouri		5						X			
Montana		8-12				1					X
Nebraska		9				1	X				
Nevada	X										X
New Hampshire											
New Jersey	X										X
New Mexico	X					1			X		X
New York		8-12				1					
North Carolina				180 ch		1	X				
North Dakota		8-12				1	X			X	
Ohio			3						X		
Oklahoma	X					1	X				
Oregon		9				1	X				
Pennsylvania	X[a]					1					
Rhode Island											
South Carolina											
South Dakota		8-12				1					
Tennessee		6-9				1				X	
Texas		8-12				1		X			
Utah	X					1	X	X			
Vermont	X	6				1					
Virginia				120 ch		2+					X
Washington		6				1	X	X			
West Virginia											
Wisconsin		8				1	X				
Wyoming		8				1+	X	X	X		

sh = semester hours
ch = clock hours
[a] Some liberal arts institutions still require only part of a semester

SOURCE: National Education Association Standards and Certification Bodies, 1983
p. 40

TABLE 61. Practicum: student teaching secondary, by state: 1983

State	Length					Type of Student Teaching					
	One Semester	Number of Weeks	Number of Quarters	Number of Hours	Varies	Number of Placements	Teaching only in Specialty	Cross level Teaching	Across Socio-economic Levels	Bilingual/ Multicultural	Varies
Alabama	X	10				1	X				
Alaska					X						X
Arizona					X						X
Arkansas											
California	X							X	X		
Colorado	X					1-2	X				
Connecticut				6-12sh							X
Delaware		15				1					
Florida		8-12				1		X	X		
Georgia	X					1	X				
Hawaii	X					1		X			
Idaho		8-12				2	X				
Illinois		6-9				1	X				
Indiana	X					1	X				
Iowa					X	1	X				
Kansas		8					X				
Kentucky		12									
Louisiana						1	X				
Maine					X						X
Maryland		8-12				1					
Massachusetts				300 ch		1-2	X				
Michigan		10				1					
Minnesota					X						X
Mississippi		6				1	X				
Missouri		5						X			
Montana		8-12				1					X
Nebraska		9				1	X				
Nevada	X										X
New Hampshire											
New Jersey	X										X
New Mexico	X					1		X			X
New York		8-12				1					X
North Carolina				180 ch							
North Dakota		8-12				1	X				
Ohio			3						X		
Oklahoma	X					1	X				
Oregon		9				1	X				
Pennsylvania	X^a					1					
Rhode Island											
South Carolina											
South Dakota		8-12				1					
Tennessee		6-9				1				X	
Texas		8-12				1		X			
Utah	X					1	X	X			
Vermont		6				1					
Virginia				120 ch		2+					X
Washington		6				1	X	X			X
West Virginia											
Wisconsin		8				1	X				
Wyoming						1+	X	X	X		

sh = semester hours
ch = clock hours
a Some liberal arts institutions still require only part of a semester

SOURCE: National Education Association, Standards and Certification Bodies, 1983, p. 41

teachers were certified to teach in some field in 1981. Seventy-eight percent were qualified to teach in the field currently assigned in 1981,[48] compared to 69 percent in 1961.[49]

Teachers in public elementary schools are more likely to be qualified to teach in their principal assignments than are teachers in secondary schools. About 90 percent of new teacher graduates in preprimary or elementary schools were qualified to teach in their principal assignments in 1981, compared to 74 percent in public secondary schools and 68 percent teaching in combined elementary/ secondary schools.[50]

New teachers in public schools are more likely to be certified to teach in their assigned field than those in private schools. Eighty-two percent of new teacher graduates in public schools were qualified to teach in the field they were assigned, compared to 70 percent in private religiously affiliated schools and 53 percent in non-religiously affiliated schools. Among new teachers in private non-religiously affiliated schools in May 1981, 23 percent lacked state certification to teach any field.[51]

TABLE 62. Certification process, by state: 1983

State	Approved Program Approach		In-State Graduates					Out-of-State Graduates								Fee
	Yes	No	Recommendations	Recommendation + Transcript	State Exam	National Teacher Examination	Other	Transcript Evaluation	Evaluation + Recommendation	Interstate Reciprocity Agreement	NCATE Program Approval	Equivalent Certificate	State Examination	National Teacher Examination	Other	
Alabama	X		X		X		X	X		X	X					$10
Alaska	X		X					X	X		X					$30
Arizona	X		X					X								$10[a]
Arkansas *																
California	X		X					X	X	X				X		$40
Colorado	X			X					X							$15
Connecticut	X			X				X	X	X						$15
Delaware	X		X						X							
Florida	X			X				X	X	X						$12
Georgia	X										X					
Hawaii		X														
Idaho	X			X				X								$20
Illinois	X		X					X								$20
Indiana	X			X				X		X	X					$ 5
Iowa	X			X				X	X				X			$15
Kansas	X		X						X							$13
Kentucky	X		X					X	X	X	X					None
Louisiana	X							X	X		X				X	None
Maine	X		X					X	X							None
Maryland	X		X					X		X	X	X				$10
Massachusetts	X			X				X	X							$10
Michigan	X		X					X	X	X	X					None
Minnesota	X			X				X								$35
Mississippi	X		X					X								None
Missouri		X[e]		X				X								
Montana	X		X					X	X	X						$20
Nebraska	X		X	X				X	X				X	X		$25
Nevada		X						X								$30
New Hampshire *																
New Jersey	X		X					X	X							$20
New Mexico	X		X	X				X								
New York	X		X					X	X							$10
North Carolina	X					X			X						X	$20
North Dakota	X		X						X							$ 5
Ohio	X		X	X					X							$ 2
Oklahoma		X	X	X	X			X	X							
Oregon	X		X						X							$25[g]
Pennsylvania	X		X					X	X							$15
Rhode Island *																
South Carolina *																
South Dakota	X		X					X	X	X						$10
Tennessee	X			X				X	X		X	X				$ 2
Texas	X		X						X							$17
Utah	X			X						X						$10
Vermont	X		X							X						$10
Virginia	X			X							X					
Washington	X			X				X		X						$15
West Virginia *																
Wisconsin	X		X					X								$30
Wyoming	X			X				X						X		

* States did not respond to survey.

SOURCE: National Education Association, <u>Standards and Certification Bodies</u>, 1983 p. 46

Standardized Examination	Teaching Experience	Other Experience	B.A. + Graduate Hours for Certification	Yes	No	Frequency of Renewal (years)	5th Year	Graduate Credits	In-service hours	Experiential Learning	Payment of Fee Only	Other	Renewal Fee	Elementary	Secondary
					X	8		X	X				$10		
	X	X			X	5		X							
			X		X	6		X					$ 5		
X				X		5					X		$40		
				X		5		X					$15		
				X											
				X		10									
					X	5		X	X				$10		
					X	7			X						
				X											
					X	5					X		$20		
					X	1					X		$ 4		
				X			X						$ 5	10 yrs	10 yrs
		X[b]			X	10		X					$15		
					X	5		X					$13		
					X	10	X						None		
					X	3						X[c]	None	3 yrs	3 yrs
					X	5			X				None		
					X	10	X	X	X			Xd	$10	10 yrs	10 yrs
				X											
				X											
					X	5							$35		
					X	5		X	X				None		
		X[f]		X											
				X											
					X	5-7		X	X				$25		
	X				X	5		X	X				$10		
					X	5-10	X	X	X					8 yrs	8 yrs
				X											
					X	5			X				$15		
					X	5		X					$ 5		
				X							X		$ 2		
					X	5			X						
					X	3-5	X	X	X				$25		6 yrs
					X	3		X				X[h]	$15	3 yrs	3 yrs
					X	5		X					$ 5		
					X	10	X	X					None		
				X											
				X											
					X	1-10[i]		X							
		X		X			X	X					$15	7 yrs	7 yrs
				X[j]				X					$30		
					X	5		X							

SUMMARY AND CONCLUSIONS

Myths abound in the public perception of education in the United States today. Even classroom teachers and other professional educators may harbor assumptions that prove totally false when checked against the realities of available, if sometimes hidden, data. One persistent, overriding danger is that we may place altogether too much faith in the concept of "national averages," for example. In truth, variations are so great among and even within the states that generalizations based on nationwide averages must be made with built-in caveats.

At least eight fundamental points jump out in any state-by-state analysis of the condition of classroom teaching in the nation:

- o Teachers' salaries differ widely from state to state and are down in relation to the totals spent on each student.

- o Teachers' salaries not only start out low but fail to grow commensurate with salaries received by other professionals.

- o We have more teachers even though there are fewer pupils.

- o Demand for teachers is starting to exceed supply and is expected to grow.

- o The caliber of new teachers is low and is getting worse.

- o The percentage of certified teachers in public schools is far greater than in private schools.

o   Federal and state contributions to school funding
     show vast differences across the country.

During the 1970s population shifts in the United States were dramatic, from the industrial Northeast and North Central regions to the "Sun Belt" South and Far West. Equally dramatic was the change in the nation's demography with the percentage of blacks increasing from 11.1 percent of the total population to almost 12 percent, and the fastest growing minority, persons of Spanish origin, going from 4.5 percent to 6.4 percent. Whites, the overwhelming majority, actually declined from 87.4 percent to 83.2 percent. Reflecting these factors, school enrollments declined most in the industrial states and actually rose in some states in the South and West. Delaware lost nearly one-third of its public school students in the last decade while Utah added over 20 percent. All minorities, while representing 17 percent of total population, comprised 26 percent of those of school age and accounted for almost half of school enrollment in several Southern and Western states.

In a nation undergoing so much change so quickly, it was small wonder that paradoxes appeared. One example: While public elementary and secondary school enrollments dropped 14 percent from 1972-73 to 1982-83, the number of teachers rose 1.4 percent and the total instructional staff increased 2.4 percent. The average teacher—about 37 years old, with 12 years' experience and a master's degree, married and with two children, white, not politically active, teaching in a suburban school—was working a little longer (an estimated 46 hours in a 180-day year) than a blue-collar worker in industry and drawing a little less pay ($20,531 on the average nationally). Most of the 1,176,711 public elementary teachers are women—981,262 to about 195,449 men, or five to one. Secondary schools show a relative balance, 474,148 women to 487,713 men.

The nation's 62,000 elementary and 24,500 secondary schools are in slightly fewer than 16,000 school districts. A typical elementary school has about 500 students, middle (or junior high) schools about 700, and senior high schools about 1,200. An elementary teacher would average about 23 pupils, and a secondary teacher would meet about five classes a day, or 121 students.

In the wide swing between salaries, Alaska is dominant at $33,953 and Mississippi at the rear with $14,285. Almost two-thirds of the states (31) pay below the national average. Furthermore, teachers' salaries, as a percentage of total spent on public and elementary schools, are slipping—from 49 percent in 1972-73 to 38 percent a decade later—even as the amount spent on each student increased by 182 percent over the period: $2,917, compared to $1,035.

Teachers' salaries at entry—$12,769 for a public elementary or secondary school beginner with a bachelor's degree — are almost $3,500 below starting pay for the next lowest professional, $16,200 for a college graduate in business administration, and considerably less than for the highest for the holder of a bachelor's degree, $20,364 in computer sciences. The worst news, however, is how the gap widens as the years go by—about $25,000 after 15 years for the teacher, $40,000 to $50,000 for, say, an accountant who started at $16,000.

Despite a total U.S. population gain of 10.6 percent in the decade, enrollment in public elementary and secondary schools shrank 14 percent, from 46,960,736 in 1972-73 to an estimated 39,505,691 in 1982-83. Some 4,961,755 are enrolled in private schools, almost all of them religiously affiliated. The decline in public school enrollments, mostly reflecting a lower birth rate, did not reduce the teacher corps. Rather, because of other demands—such as to lower teacher-to-pupil ratios and provide more facilities for handicapped students—the number of teachers grew by 1.4 percent, from 2,108,846 in 1972-73 to 2,138,572 in 1982-83.

Still, the demand continues to exceed the supply. According to the National Center for Education Statistics, the country will need 8,000 more teacher graduates in 1983 than it will get, 4,000 more next year, 28,000 the year after, 31,000 in 1986, and 15,000 in 1987. Less than 5 percent of high school seniors headed for college say they want to major in education, a 50 percent drop from 1973. The annual supply of new teacher graduates is down from 314,000 in 1971 to 132,000 in 1981. As a percentage of bachelor's degrees, new teacher graduates fell from 37 percent in 1971 to 12 percent in 1981.

Never before in the nation's history has the caliber of those entering the teaching profession been as low as it is today. Scores of high school seniors taking the 1982 Scholastic Aptitude Tests showed those choosing education as a major fell well below those entering the arts, the biological sciences, business, commerce and communications, physical sciences, and social sciences. This was true for every state in the union. Teaching, clearly, is not attracting America's best minds.

And yet, public school teachers seem held to a higher standard than those in private schools. More are certified to teach in the fields currently assigned them than ever before: 82 percent in public schools qualified to teach what they are teaching, compared to 70 percent in private, religiously affiliated schools, and 53 percent in private, non-religiously affilated schools. Among new teachers in the latter, 23 percent lacked certification in any field.

The great disparity among the 50 states and the District of Columbia was nowhere stronger than in the degree of support from outside the local jurisdictions. The federal government contributed 23 percent of the Mississippi budget for public elementary and secondary schools in 1982-83, for example, and only 3.5 percent in New Jersey. In Hawaii, the state's contribution was 90 percent. In California, it was 86 percent. But in New Hampshire, the state gave only 9 percent, with the local jurisdiction putting up 89 percent (compared to 1 percent in Hawaii).

SOURCES OF DATA

While the basic data used for this report were obtained from many sources, the compilation and analyses are original. General population numbers were obtained from several documents published by the U.S. Department of Commerce, Bureau of the Census, and Bureau of Economic Analysis. Public school enrollments, numbers of teachers, salaries of teachers, and expenditures and revenues were obtained from the National Education Association (because NEA has the most current data available). Private school enrollment data were obtained from the National Catholic Education Association and the National Center for Education Statistics. Personal income and per-capita income figures came from the U.S. Department of Commerce, Bureau of Economic Analysis. The U.S. Department of Labor, Bureau of Labor Statistics provided salary data for professions other than teaching. Basic data concerning who is going into teaching and qualifications of new teacher graduates were obtained from the U.S. Department of Education, National Center for Education Statistics and the National Education Association. The College Entrance Examination Board provided Scholastic Aptitude Test (SAT) data for each state. Teacher certification data were obtained from a survey we conducted among the states, the Council of Chief State School Officers and the National Education Association.

NOTES

1. Computed from National Education Association (NEA), <u>Estimates of School Statistics 1982-83</u> (Washington: January 1983), p. 11; NEA, <u>Estimates of School Statistics 1973-74</u> (Washington: 1974), p. 8; U.S. Department of Commerce, Bureau of Economic Analysis, <u>Commerce News, Report BEA #83-21</u> (Washington: U.S. Department of Commerce, May 1983), table 4; and U.S. Department of Commerce, Bureau of the Census, <u>Statistical Abstract of the United States,</u> 103rd Edition (Washington: U.S. Government Printing Office, 1983), p. 12.

2. Computed from Bureau of Economic Analysis, <u>U.S. Department of Commerce News,</u> May 2, 1983, Table 4; and U.S. Department of Commerce, Bureau of the Census, <u>Statistical Abstract of the United States,</u> 1982-83, p. 12.

3. Bureau of Economic Analysis, <u>U.S. Department of Commerce News,</u> May 2, 1983, Table 4.

4. U.S. Bureau of the Census, <u>1980 Census of Population, Supplementary report, Race of the Population by States: 1980</u> (Washington: U.S. Government Printing Office, July 1981) pp. 8-11.

5. <u>Ibid.,</u> p. 1.

6. U.S. Bureau of the Census, <u>1980 Census of Population, Supplementary Report, Persons of Spanish Origin by State: 1980,</u> (Washington: U.S. Government Printing Office, August 1982) p. 1.

7. U.S. Bureau of the Census, Race of the Population by States: 1980, p. 1.

8. Computed from National Education Association, Estimates of School Statistics 1982-83, p. 11.

9. Harold Hodgkinson, "What's Still Right With Education," Phi Delta Kappan, December 1982, p. 233.

10. "Invasion from Mexico: It Just Keeps Growing," U.S. News and World Report, March 7, 1983, p. 37.

11. U.S. Department of Education, National Center for Educational Statistics, The Condition of Education: 1983 (Washington: U.S. Government Printing Office, 1983), p. 18.

12. National Catholic Education Association, United States Catholic Elementary and Secondary Schools 1982-83, p. 6.

13. National Education Association, Estimates of School Statistics 1982-83, pp. 14, 15.

14. Feistritzer Associates, The American Teacher, Feistritzer Publications, 1983, p. 1.

15. Ibid., p. 3.

16. Ibid., p. 3.

17. National Education Association, Status of the American Public School Teacher, 1980-81, p. 64.

18. _Ibid._, p. 95.

19. U.S. Department of Education, National Center for Education Statistics, The Condition of Education 1982 (Washington: 1982), pp. 93, 95.

20. U.S. Department of education, National Center for Education Statistics, Projections of Education Statistics 1990-91 (Washington: 1982), vol. 1, p. 21.

21. National Education Association, Status of the American Public School Teacher, 1980-81, p. 59.

22. _Ibid._, p. 73-78.

23. National Education Association, Estimates of School Statistics 1982-83, p. 21.

24. Education Commission of the States, School Finance Reform in the States: 1983, p. 18.

25. U.S. Department of Commerce, Bureau of the Census, Statistical Abstract of the United States 1982-83 (Washington: 1982), p. 25.

26. National Education Association, Prices, Budgets, Salaries and Income, February 1983, p. 24.

27. Interview, U.S. Department of Labor, Bureau of Labor Statistics, June 24, 1983.

28. U.S. Department of Education, Projections of Education Statistics 1990-1991, pp. 21-22.

29. U.S. Department of Education, Condition of Education: 1983, p. 176.

30. _Ibid._, p. 176.

31. College Entrance Examination Board, _National College-Bound Seniors, 1982_, pp. 9, 10.

32. U.S. Department of Education, National Center for Education Statistics, _Special Report_, February 1982, p. 1.

33. U.S. Department of Education. _Condition of Education: 1983_, p. 182.

34. _Ibid._, p. 172.

35. U.S. Department of Education: _Projections of Education Statistics 1990-91_, p. 71.

36. Feistritzer Associates, _The American Teacher_, p. 23.

37. U.S. Department of Education, National Center for Education Statistics, _Digest of Education Statistics 1982_, p. 93.

38. U.S. Department of Education, _The Condition of Education: 1983_, pp. 172, 173.

39. _Ibid._, p. 190.

40. Feistritzer Associates, _The American Teacher_, p. 59.

41. T. M. Stinnet, _A Manual on Certification Requirement for School Personnel in the United States_ (Washington: National Education Association, 1970), p. 27.

42. Task Force on Approved Programs, Florida Association of Colleges for Teacher Education, "Quality Performance-Based Program Approval, A New Approach to Approved Programs for Educational Personnel in Florida" (Draft), pp. 3, 4.

43. Carol Lewis, Educational Governance in the States, U.S. Department of Education, February 1983, p. 115.

44. Ibid.

45. William E. Gardner and John R. Palmer, "Certification Accreditation: Background, Issue Analysis and Recommendation," background paper submitted to National Commission on Excellance in Education, August 1982, pp. 24-29.

46. Report of the Council of Chief State School Officers' Ad Hoc Committee on Teacher Certification, Preparation and Accreditation, Washington, D.C., July 1982, pp. 35, 43.

47. Lewis, Educational Goverance in the States, p. 115.

48. U.S. Department of Education, The Condition of Education: 1983, p. 176.

49. National Education Association, Status of the American Public School Teacher, p. 40.

50. U.S. Department of Education, The National Education Association, The Condition of Education: 1983, p. 176.

51. Ibid.